How to Become an Influencer

How to Earn Substantial Money Online to Take Control of Your Life

(How to Build a Personal Brand With Strategic Social Media Marketing)

John Saad

Published By **Andrew Zen**

John Saad

How to Become an Influencer: How to Earn Substantial Money Online to Take Control of Your Life (How to Build a Personal Brand With Strategic Social Media Marketing)

ISBN   978-1-998901-81-4

No part of this guidbook shall be reproduced in any form without permission in writing from the publisher except in the case of brief quotations embodied in critical articles or reviews.

Legal & Disclaimer

The information contained in this book is not designed to replace or take the place of any form of medicine or professional medical advice. The information in this book has been provided for educational & entertainment purposes only.

The information contained in this book has been compiled from sources deemed reliable, and it is accurate to the best of the Author's knowledge; however, the Author cannot guarantee its accuracy and validity and cannot be held liable for any errors or omissions. Changes are periodically made to this book. You must consult your doctor or get professional medical advice before using any of the suggested remedies, techniques, or information in this book.

Table of Contents

Chapter 1: Finding Your Niche

Focusing on a specific trouble or area of understanding that you could provide at the side of your fans is a way to find out your place of interest as an Instagram influencer. The subjects right here might also range from tour, cuisine, and fitness to fashion and splendor. By figuring out your region of interest, you could function your self as a topic-rely authority and amass a committed following of those who are keen to pay interest what you have got were given to mention.

Consider your regions of hobby and what you can offer that is specific and useful on your goal market as an area to begin at the same time as seeking to recognize your vicinity of hobby.

Additionally, reflect onconsideration on the material you like producing and the kinds of matters that your target market famous compelling. Researching what issues and instructions are currently trending on Instagram further to any holes in the market that you could cope with may be beneficial.

To create a community round your understanding, you need to additionally make the effort to have interaction your fans. By doing so, you may characteristic your self as a leader to your enterprise, get greater fanatics, and seize more opportunities.

What do you've got got understanding in and are enthusiastic about? Pick a topic or problem that you may address and growth cloth round.

It might be tough but profitable to find your area of interest as an Instagram influencer. To help you in identifying your strong point, undergo in thoughts the subsequent steps:

Consider your passions and regions of interest: What do you glaringly gravitate within the direction of? What subjects are you inquisitive about studying approximately and discussing with others? You want to pick out out a topic that you are captivated with thinking about the reality that it's miles going to be much less complex a great manner to supply content material and have interaction with your audience.

Find out who your competitors are: Look at the subjects that incredible influencers for your possible place are strolling a weblog about. You'll get a experience of the troubles which can be trending and the information this is already to be had from this.

Determine your unique perspective: What distinguishes you from other influencers on your problem? How are you able to method your area of interest from a unique mind-set?

Examine severa niches: You aren't required to pick out a speciality right now right away. Examine many subject topics in your posts to find which of them hook up with your readers.

Reduce your interest: Start that specialize in a positive place after you've got got have been given a deeper knowledge of what appeals to you and your goal market. You will gain a devoted following and solidify your function as an authority for your problem if you try this.

Keep in thoughts that setting up your sturdy issue is a way, and it's far pinnacle to discover and exchange your thoughts alongside the way.

The maximum vital issue is to be reliable to who you are and bring stuff that you are captivated with.

How People Fail In Finding A Niche As An Instagram Influencer

When trying to carve out a gap as an Instagram influencer, customers regularly make the following mistakes:

Not knowledge who their audience is: Knowing who you are attempting to acquire along with your fabric is critical. Making content material material that appeals to absolutely everyone is probably difficult with out a smooth purpose marketplace in thoughts.

Failure to specialize: There is a lot of opposition on Instagram, and if you are not concentrated on a positive region of knowledge, it might be hard to stand out. You can also furthermore gain a dedicated following via way of specializing on a superb difficulty or area of interest.

Not being actual: It's essential to be sincere and actual on your writing. Building consider along side your fanatics and preserving a devoted following may be tough in case you are not sincere.

Being inconsistent: To gain a following on Instagram, consistency is important. Keeping your lovers involved might be hard if you do now not post frequently or in case your fabric is inconsistent along side your principal aspect.

Not engaging together with your fans on Instagram: Instagram is a social net web page, consequently it's miles critical to connect with your followers there. Building a robust community and increasing your following is probably hard in case you are not connecting collectively together with your fanatics.

Benefits Of Having The Best Niche As An Instagram Influencer

As an Instagram influencer, sticking to 1 place of knowledge might be effective for the subsequent motives:

You may furthermore boom a committed and devoted goal marketplace by the usage of becoming location of interest precise: You may also draw a following who are inquisitive about that difficulty and are greater inclined to interact together with your fabric via manner of concentrated on that undertaking depend.

It may additionally moreover want to make it much less complicated as a way to monetise your account: Companies and corporations are often interested in taking factor with influencers who've a specific following and have the functionality to attain a high quality demographic of potential customers. Finding sponsorships and partnerships that complement your content cloth and goal market may be less hard if you have a properly defined robust point.

It permits you to enlarge your authority to your organization: You might also feature yourself as a geared up and dependable deliver of statistics to your corporation thru often providing terrific fabric concerning your knowledge. This may additionally moreover open up greater doors for speaking engagements, joint ventures, and awesome techniques to monetize your have an effect on.

It makes it less complex a good way to distinguish your self from the competition considering there are such a number of Instagram influencers. You might also set your self apart from top notch influencers and draw a different and engaged following with the useful aid of concentrated on a superb difficulty rely.

Chapter 2: Using High-Quality Images And Videos

To have interaction and draw on your target marketplace as an influencer on Instagram, you want to employ pinnacle charge photographs and movies. Here are some hints for the usage of pinnacle charge images and motion photographs on Instagram:

Use a first-rate virtual camera: To take clear, specific photos and films, spend money on an excellent digital camera or a cellphone with a tremendous digital camera.

Utilize natural lighting fixtures: Use herbal lights to provide properly-lit and aesthetically appealing photos and films.

Edit your photos: To enhance the colors, lighting, and stylish look of your photos, use picture enhancing software program.

Use extremely good video: Use a terrific virtual camera at the equal time as making films, and make sure the photograph is sharp and properly-lit.

Pay interest to composition: Composition describes the arrangement of the additives in a photo or video. Pay near interest to the subjects' positioning inside the frame and the concord of the empty region.

You can produce extraordinary images and films an notable manner to make you stand out as an Instagram influencer through the usage of those guidelines. Make nice your cloth is properly-written and captivating to the eye. Purchase a pleasant digital camera or a smartphone with a pleasant digital camera, and think about making use of photo-enhancing software program software program to beautify your photographs.

Benefits Of Using High Quality Images And Videos

Instagram influencers can also get loads of advantages through using brilliant pictures and movement snap shots, which encompass:

Better engagement: High-amazing images and films are more likely to trap the eye of your followers and convince them to love, declaration, and percentage your fabric. Your obtain and everyday platform engagement may moreover moreover every advantage from this.

Enhanced credibility: Using notable pictures and motion photos can also assist to area you as a dependable and terrific influencer. This is mainly essential in case you're searching out to negotiate sponsored content material fabric material partnerships with companies.

Better logo example: High-excellent pics and movies also can assist to venture a greater polished and professional picture in case you're the use of Instagram to sell your non-public or commercial emblem. By doing this, you will be capable of benefit the target audience's recognize and credibility.

Enhanced storytelling: High splendid snap shots and films may be an effective device for storytelling, permitting you to offer your factor in a manner that is each aesthetically attractive and persuasive.

Greater emblem enchantment: Brands regularly are attempting to find out influencers to have interaction with who offer cloth of a immoderate super. Employing top-notch pics and films will help you stand out to potential commercial organisation partners and decorate your possibilities of landing sponsored content material cloth opportunities.

What Not To Do When Using High Quality Images And Videos

When utilising exquisite snap shots and films as an Instagram influencer, there are some belongings you have to live faraway from:

Verify that you have permission to apply any photos or motion pix earlier than posting them in your Instagram account to keep away from breaking copyright felony pointers. To use any content material fabric covered with the aid of manner of copyright, you have to get the specified licenses or lets in.

Posting poorly made or significantly changed cloth isn't always perfect. It's OK to use minimum adjustments on your pics and movies, however attempt to chorus from overly manipulating them just so they seem synthetic or unnatural. It's critical to be sincere and actual at the side of your audience.

Avoid the use of filters or outcomes excessively: While they may be a remarkable tool to beautify your material, avoid the use of them so often that they turn out to be a distraction from the content material cloth itself.

Don't neglect the caption: Your Instagram post's caption is critical, so ensure to give it a few interest. To upload fee to your article, try and stay a ways from common or unoriginal captions and try to embody context or thrilling facts.

Don't forget about about to have interaction along side your audience: As an influencer, it's far important to have interaction in conjunction with your aim market and reply to messages and feedback. Failure to achieve this could in all likelihood purpose a rift together together along with your fanatics and undermine your authority as an influencer.

Mistake Influencers Make When Using High Quality Images And Videos

Influencers that located up notable images and films on Instagram threat making the following errors:

Having little regard for his or her site visitors When selecting content cloth fabric, it's far essential to take your purpose market's tastes and hobbies beneath attention. Striking a balance among fantastic and relevancy is essential for the reason that high wonderful pix and films may not continuously be attractive for your target market.

Leaving out the caption: The caption is an crucial problem of an Instagram placed up because it offers context and engages the viewer. The impact of the amazing photo or video might be faded if the caption is not noted or is written poorly.

Excessive improving: While it is vital to painting material in the outstanding moderate feasible, excessive enhancing might probable cause it to seem synthetic and unreal. Finding a balance between the usage of filters and editing sparingly is essential.

Not the use of hashtags may moreover restriction the purpose market for your fabric and make it more hard for customers to find out it. The achieve of your material may be decreased in case you fail to encompass pertinent hashtags.

Not updating frequently: Maintaining and developing an Instagram following calls for ordinary posting. Regular posting is crucial to maintain your target audience inquisitive about your material and engaged.

Chapter 3: Engaging With Your Audience

Engaging at the side of your target audience as an Instagram influencer entails communicating immediately with individuals who observe and have interaction together with your posts.

Using Instagram's system like Instagram Live and IGTV to engage together at the side of your fans in real-time might also help you do this. It also can contain reacting to comments, like and commenting on one-of-a-kind clients' posts.

As an Instagram influencer, you could have interaction together collectively along with your audience in a whole lot of strategies, together with the subsequent:

Make an try and respond to remarks to your posts, specially individuals who ask questions or demand an answer. This encourages a enjoy of network among your lovers and suggests them how hundreds you respect their participation.

Utilize Instagram's functions. Instagram has some of gadget that allow you to speak collectively along with your lovers in actual time, which encompass Instagram Live and

IGTV. Utilize those gadget to answer queries from enthusiasts, provide within the decrease again of-the-scenes information, and interact in more intimate communique.

Work collectively with unique customers: Working collectively with other customers, specially those who have an audience this is just like yours, is a high-quality opportunity to have interaction with that audience and amplify your acquire. To help each unique's growth, you could percentage an additional's content material material, run contests or giveaways, or work collectively to create content fabric.

Request enter: Getting to apprehend your target market better and analyzing what they want to look from you can every be executed through manner of soliciting for feedback from them. You may also request feedback thru feedback, personal messages, or Instagram polls and surveys.

Building a dating with the individuals who help and study your art work is the general aim of connecting together together with your goal marketplace as an Instagram influencer. You can construct a devoted and engaged target market on your material by way of the usage of actively attractive with them and listening to their input.

It's crucial to have interaction together collectively along with your fans on Instagram as it's a social media internet site online. In order to enhance your material, respond to comments and direct messages and solicit feedback.

The Extent You Should Go In Engaging With Audience

In order to develop a strong network and sell a brilliant enterprise organization image, it is crucial for Instagram influencers to interact with their fans. We already recognise that this will encompass answering messages and feedback, retweeting and commenting on posts from your fanatics, and soliciting pointers for reinforcing your fabric.

Setting limits and looking after your very non-public wishes are as vital, however. It is OK to take pauses or assign a part of the technique to a crew if required because of the reality that trying to keep up with every single remark and message is probably onerous. Furthermore, it's vital to hold in thoughts which you don't want to fulfill all of your fans' needs or clear up all in their problems, and you can installation limitations for a way an lousy lot interaction you have with them.

The diploma to which you have interaction together together with your goal marketplace in the long run is based upon on your targets, available belongings, and personal options. It's vital to strike a stability that blessings each you and your target audience.

Pros And Cons Of Engaging With Audience As An Instagram Influencer

Being an Instagram influencer has each benefits and disadvantages in terms of target market engagement. Consider the following blessings and downsides:

Pros:

Establishing a community: Interacting on the facet of your intention marketplace may additionally moreover furthermore help you set up a community of dedicated supporters who're obsessed with your message and content material.

Increasing your visibility: Since Instagram's set of tips favors cloth that generates interaction, you could placed it to use in your gain with the aid of the use of responding to remarks and speaking with particular customers.

Increasing your impact: By interacting together with your audience, you can end up recognized as an professional on your trouble and increase your impact as an influencer.

Gaining expertise: Talking collectively together with your goal marketplace might also provide you beneficial facts about what your enthusiasts are interested by and a way to make your fabric greater enticing.

Cons:

Time-consuming: Communicating on the aspect of your target market takes time, mainly if you have a giant fan base.

Negative feedback: You may additionally additionally every so often should cope with terrible or crucial feedback considering the fact that now not all remarks may be favorable.

Managing expectancies: As a give up end result of your engagement collectively along side your aim marketplace, you may want to manage their expectations as well. Be careful no longer to over promise or underdeliver in your cloth.

Personal statistics: It's essential to be cautious whilst disclosing personal data considering attractive at the side of your target market can also disclose you to facts you do now not want to show.

Chapter 4: Using Hashtags

As an Instagram influencer, the use of hashtags also can expand your following and make your publish greater visible. When you embody a hashtag in an Instagram publish, it turns into clickable, permitting human beings to search for and find greater posts that still include the identical hashtag.

By doing this, you could make connections with folks who percentage your hobbies in positive topics or thoughts and growth the opportunity that clients who do now not already comply with you may gain this.

As an Instagram influencer, it's vital to pick out hashtags which can be appropriate in your target market and content in case you need to make use of hashtags efficiently. You might also moreover additionally blend drastically used big hashtags (like #instagood or #touring) with extra specialised hashtags (like #travelblogger or #foodphotography). To entice your enthusiasts to utilize it at the same time as tweeting about your devices or offerings, you can additionally create your non-public hashtag.

It's essential to keep away from overusing hashtags while using them as an Instagram influencer. Too many hashtags can also make your content material seem spammy or maybe decrease engagement. Use no more than 30 hashtags every publish, as a favored rule of thumb.

As an Instagram influencer, hashtags can also moreover assist you benefit a larger target marketplace and make your post extra seen. To maximize the blessings, simply be cautious to select pertinent hashtags and make use of them correctly.

By making it easier for clients to find your cloth, hashtags help your content fabric accumulate a bigger audience. To make your content material cloth cloth extra visible, embody pertinent hashtags.

Types Of Instagram Hashtags And How To Use Them

Instagram hashtags allow clients to tag their posts at the same time as additionally permitting distinctive customers to find material that is applicable to awesome phrases or subjects. The caption of a post or the remarks area can also every encompass hashtags.

You may additionally furthermore use some of one-of-a-kind varieties of Instagram hashtags, which includes:

Popular hashtags are those which might be often used by masses of humans. The hashtags "love," "instagood," and "tbt" are examples (Throwback Thursday).

Niche hashtags are those that are unique to a certain scenario, issue rely, or place of the net. Consider the hashtags for culinary pix, excursion, and motivational fitness.

Place-specific hashtags: These encompass the name of a place, which includes a city, state, or landmark. #newyorkcity, #bali, or #eiffeltower are a few examples.

Hashtags for manufacturers: These are particular to a fantastic emblem or product. Nike, Apple, or Starbucks are a few examples.

Hashtags for campaigns: These are hashtags which might be particular to a marketing advertising marketing campaign or event. The #metgala, #oscars, or #worldcup, as an example.

To use Instagram hashtags successfully, you should:

Use pertinent hashtags: Rather than depending excellent on trending hashtags which may be unrelated on your article, use hashtags which might be associated for your subject matter.

Use a aggregate of trending and vicinity of expertise hashtags: Trending hashtags also can help you connect to individuals who are inquisitive about extraordinary topics or issues, while area of interest hashtags can help you attain a bigger purpose marketplace.

Use quite a number hashtags: Avoid reusing a small quantity of hashtags. Change subjects round to ensure you're task a number of human beings.

Use moderation at the same time as the use of hashtags. Instagram permits as much as 30 steady with put up, however along with too many may make your placed up seem spammy and flip off customers. Limit yourself to a select few hashtags which might be relevant on your content material cloth material.

Pros And Cons Of Using Hashtags As An Influencer On Instagram

As an Instagram influencer, using hashtags may additionally additionally help you attain a larger goal marketplace and growth the publicity of your submit. However, there are benefits and disadvantages of employing hashtags to don't forget.

Pros:

You may additionally additionally hook up with extra people with the useful resource of the use of hashtags: Your material might be more without problems located through visitors who're seeking out sure key terms or topics in case you utilize relevant hashtags on your postings.

You may additionally additionally discover folks who percentage your pursuits with the aid of manner of manner of using hashtags: You may additionally moreover interact with others who have similar pastimes to yours via the usage of manner of using certain hashtags. This can be an effective approach for developing a following for your work.

You may additionally use hashtags to degree the effectiveness of your content material fabric fabric: It might be useful to evaluate how effectively your fabric is connecting along with your goal marketplace if you may degree the general standard overall performance of your content material fabric fabric by means of hashtag the use of one of the many social media analytics device to be had.

Cons:

It's viable to use hashtags excessively. Using excessive portions of hashtags in postings may probably pop out as spammy to advantageous humans. Only use hashtags which may be applicable on your publish and use them sparingly.

Hashtags may be abused thru high great customers as a way to control the device and increase the exposure in their data. Users seeking out positive hashtags may also moreover get a crowded and spammy feed as a result.

Using too many hashtags in a submit may additionally moreover detract from the content material material itself and make it extra difficult for traffic to understand the important elements you are trying to precise.

Overall, hashtags can be a beneficial device for Instagram influencers, but to maximise their effectiveness, it's miles essential to apply them sparingly and strategically.

Chapter 5: Collaborating With Other Creators And Brands

In order to expand and distribute content material fabric that is at the same time useful, Instagram influencers ought to collaborate with one-of-a-kind artists and corporations. This also can take place in lots of strategies, like:

Sponsored posts: An influencer receives fee from a business enterprise to sell that brand's items or offerings thru a located up on that influencer's Instagram page.

Collaboration among an influencer and a logo effects in cloth that highlights every activities. This is probably a image consultation, movie, or one-of-a-type piece of content material that promotes the influencer and the enterprise organisation concurrently.

Affiliate advertising and advertising: When an influencer promotes a emblem's items or services, they will be paid a charge for each transaction that results from their unique affiliate link.

Influencers may also furthermore boom their target marketplace and attain whilst additionally monetizing their Instagram money owed with the resource of the use of going for walks with extraordinary artists and companies. It will also be a way for businesses to market it their gadgets and offerings to new clients. Influencers ought to collaborate with companies and artists whose values they percentage a excellent way to benefit success in the ones partnerships. Influencers need to also be open and real to themselves.

The Limit You Should Go When Collaborating With Other Brands And Creators As An Instagram Influencer

Being open and honest about any partnerships you've got got with other businesses or artists is vital in case you want to achieve success as an Instagram influencer. This consists of revealing any sponsored posts or alliances in compliance with the Federal Trade Commission's (FTC) necessities for testimonials and endorsements.

The FTC states which you are required to say any big dating you may have with the creator or brand you're endorsing. A fee, gift, or extraordinary shape of remuneration is an instance of a material link.

Being real and honest for your partnerships is surely as critical as reporting any monetary ties. Because they appreciate your ideas and insights, your target market respects you and follows you. It's important to hold that respect by way of manner of simplest endorsing objects and services which you in fact trust in and maintain to excessive ideals.

Last but not least, it's miles critical to preserve the overall stability of your fabric in mind and avoid letting subsidized articles or partnerships take over your feed. It's essential to strike a stability among sponsored material and your personal true content material considering the fact that your intention market follows you due to your very own point of view and voice.

Pros And Cons Of Collaborating With Other Creators And Brands As An Instagram Influencer

As an Instagram influencer, there are numerous advantages and downsides to keep in mind even as working with precise artists and companies.

Pros:

A larger purpose marketplace can be reached and your publicity on Instagram may be elevated with the resource of on foot with other manufacturers and corporations.

Opportunities for networking: Working with one in all a kind artists and groups also can assist you meet people to your vicinity and research from them.

Content that is of a better fine may be produced thru collaboration with other manufacturers and corporations, which you could no longer were able to do in your personal.

Potential for economic praise: A lot of firms are eager to pay influencers for partnerships, which may be a precious supply of income for your company.

Cons:

Loss of manipulate: When operating with different companies and artists, you may ought to give up part of your control over your message and content cloth.

Collaboration with too many groups and artists runs the danger of muddying your personal logo, making it greater tough for your enthusiasts to realize what you stand for.

Time-eating: Working with unique artists and groups might also take time due to the fact you may want to plot meetings, brainstorm thoughts, and produce content material fabric collectively.

Potential for damage to recognition: Working with a brand or revolutionary whose ideals are at odds with yours might be poor for your repute.

As a prevent end result, operating with one in all a kind artists and companies may be a outstanding manner to boom your Instagram following and even earn money, however it's essential to cautiously weigh the blessings and disadvantages and quality work with brands and creators that percentage your beliefs.

Chapter 6: Finding Clients And Pitching

Reaching out to agencies or companies that can be interested in teaming up with you to promote their gadgets or offerings for your Instagram fans is a part of coming across clients and pitching to them as an Instagram influencer. This could in all likelihood encompass making sponsored fabric, which include articles or posts that focus the logo's goods, or maintaining giveaways or competitions to your account.

You also can do studies to locate businesses or producers that in shape your interests and style an excellent way to enchantment to clients. Then, you can contact those companies or producers proper now through Instagram or electronic mail to talk approximately a likely cooperation. When creating a presentation to prospective clients, it is vital to concisely describe the charge you can provide and the manner your target audience fits with their goal market. Along with any applicable experience or competencies you may have, you have to be organized to speak about your Instagram gain and engagement.

Actively searching out possibilities thru social media and superb on line systems is one technique to draw clients as an Instagram influencer and market your skills. To get you began out, consider the following advice:

Determine your purpose marketplace in advance than you start pitching functionality clients. You need to moreover preserve in thoughts the kinds of producers or companies you want to address. This will permit you to customize your pitch and make sure that your aim market will locate it compelling.

Increase your internet visibility: It's crucial to have a dependable and strong on-line presence for you to draw in capability customers. This includes having a professionally designed and charming Instagram account, similarly to a internet net website or on line portfolio that highlights your art work and builds your very private logo.

Use hashtags and join applicable Instagram businesses to enhance the publicity of your located up and make it much much less complex for capacity clients to find out you.

Join applicable Instagram organizations and have interaction with different influencers and enterprise people to assemble connections and perhaps discover new opportunities.

Speak with functionality clients: Reach out to the manufacturers and companies you want to collaborate with after you've got a smooth idea of their tendencies. Sending them emails or direct messages is likewise an choice, as is leaving remarks on their articles expressing your want to collaborate with them. Make wonderful to spell out your qualifications in element and display samples of your in advance work.

Follow up: If after your first touch you do now not pay interest once more from a ability customer, do not be hesitant to comply with up. While being aware about their wishes and busy schedules, it is crucial to be chronic.

Always be courteous and expert while presenting your offerings, and be open to remarks and tips from capability clients. You can be a hit as an Instagram influencer if you paintings tough and are chronic.

1

PICKING A NICHE

T

he first step to becoming an influencer is choosing which vicinity you need to influence. After all, it won't be easy to end up a football influencer if you've in no way kicked a ball for your lifestyles.

A niche is exactly that, the point of interest of your Instagram. For example, for lots models that might be splendor/modeling, however one in all a kind niches like meals and business company are just as well-known. Don't melancholy if you're no longer the most conventionally adorable individual around every, all you will need is ardour and an capability to take real virtual camera images.

There are a pair elements that you need to consider whilst figuring out which location of hobby you need to interest on:

Popularity

You need humans to comply with you in order that you'll be an influencer. Maybe you recognize masses about the 53rd mecha that seemed inside the extraordinarily-modern-day Gundam series, however how many people is that during all chance to draw? While tremendous, fantastic human beings be successful with a bargain tons much less than famous niches, this is quite now not going, and a large quantity of their fanatics are handiest following "for the lols" in choice to real hobby, which makes their community engagement low.

Instead of this, you should awareness on something it honestly is fairly famous. Maybe you're actual at video video games? You might likely apprehend numerous online game minutiae, or perhaps trivialities from a unmarried undertaking. Maybe you're a super stylist? Now, your place of hobby does now not need to be some element you are right at. For example, meals influencers do not continuously make their very own meals , but they do an incredible task of angling their pictures efficiently and writing appealing critiques.

With that being said, how do you comprehend if a few difficulty is famous? Just due to the truth a few problem is hip in your buddy circle, doesn't mean it's popular international. The first component you could take a look at is via manner of putting in the hashtag on Instagram. So, if you want to start being a food influencer, you'd input "#food" and take a look at how many consequences there are.

The second technique involves using Google traits. This net internet page will save you a whole lot of time in relation to deciding on out things which is probably currently trending and those which might be going away.

All in all, you need to search for niches which is probably quite well-known, however do now not have too many influencers either. You'll have a difficult time becoming a beauty influencer a number of the numerous hundreds of them already available. On the alternative hand, if you can predict that a few element becomes well-known soon, then you may have a head start on each person else. By becoming the first influencer for some detail, every body that appears for it on Instagram will flock to yours. Naturally, you aren't very possibly to be the number one, however typically you need to look for a gap that has a deficit of content material, in evaluation to people which might be inquisitive about the content material fabric. The critical query you must ask your self is 'how can I add fee to this area of interest?'. Making a dwelling as an influencer is all approximately such as fee

How Suitable Are You For It?

Now, I'm now not going to tell you which you need to be Messi to start a soccer Instagram. On the other hand, it might be helpful if you had some functionality with the ball, or at the least a tremendous quantity of knowledge.

You want your location of interest to both be some thing you're right at, or a few factor you may make appearance applicable. For instance, you don't need to be real at making food to be a meals blogger, however you do want to be proper at staking out locations which have thrilling-looking meals, and taking pictures of it.

Make sure you understand what your Instagram relies on in advance than selecting your vicinity of interest, because of the truth in case you're lousy at that, you gained't be having thousands success.

Passion

This is the most crucial detail even as identifying your area of interest. You acquired't emerge as well-known in a unmarried day, so you'll want to ensure which you're captivated with your problem remember, due to the fact you'll be working on it for a while.

Maintaining hobby with out a good deal incentive isn't the very first-class issue within the worldwide, this is why you want to make certain you're tremendously captivated with your niche. It can't be some issue you're 'eh' about, it wishes to be something that makes you flow into crazy!

These 3 factors are effects the maximum critical component about putting in your blog. After all, in case you get your area of interest incorrect, not anything else truely subjects, and you'll be stuck in mediocrity for some time.

Can I first-rate have one place of hobby?

You don't need to have exceptional one location of hobby! Your Instagram might also have a pair special niches on the same time. I'd suggest that all of them examine the three factors above, moreover, you want they all to provide off the identical "vibe." So you don't need to be doing rock stay general overall performance analysis together with calming pics. You want to make certain that your niches supplement each one in all a kind, in preference to going in opposition to themselves.

Now, while I've already stated some niches being a bit too famous to interrupt into, there are a few exceptions to this:

Luxury Travel- While there are various tour blogs, the high priced tour blogs which may be there, can best find out hundreds of the remarkable area that being wealthy offers you.

Modelling/Cosplay- Modelling and cosplay in this situation, only observe to women. While there are limitless quite women doing this already, new ones appear to pop up each few days, so in case you've were given some rockin' relevant seems(or virtually makeup abilities.) This may be the road for you.

With this in mind, you have to have narrowed your vicinity of hobby down, and are prepared to take the following step in your journey.

2

TAKING THE FIRST STEP

T

his financial ruin will attention on topics, the first is exploring the benefits you have got from considered certainly one of a type beginning positions(eg. Being from an person united states, being rich and so forth.) And how the ones might also have an impact on your influencing adventure. In the identical vein, we'll be exploring the wonderful options to get you started out on a charge range, collectively with studying some virtual digital camera tool that you will be using.

First of all, permit's test some topics that can make your begin hundreds much less difficult:

1. Being a girl- Influencing, on Instagram as a minimum, is a very female-ruled enterprise. On common, you'll discover that girls spend extra time on Instagram than men do. Naturally, distinct women are much less hard to relate to girls than guys are. This method that lady influencers have a strong side on guys proper right here. Many guys furthermore have the vintage thoughts-set that it isn't suitable to be following male influencers, giving ladies even greater of a dominant share.

2. Being first rate searching- Let's not mince phrases right here, being pretty allows out hundreds at the same time as becoming an influencer. It's quite much like being a film celebrity. Sure, common-looking or possibly ugly ones exist, however the subject is specifically made of handsome human beings. After all, people like searching at a quite face. If you're applicable looking, attempt to insert your self into a number of your snap shots, even though they're not your primary niche.

3. Being rich- Wealth will let you no longer satisfactory get the exceptional digital camera device spherical, it'll also allow you get right of access to to greater advertising and marketing and advertising, and connections that could make your lifestyles less hard. You moreover have plenty extra niches setting out as much as you, including pricey adventure(or nicely, adventure in cutting-edge day.)

4. Having a recognition- By this I mean, "People knew me before I began Instagram." For example, famous YouTubers, or even that guy that had his name within the papers that one time. These topics provide you with a head start, and assist you circumvent the hardest thing about turning into an influencer- getting your initial goal market.

5. Coming from a well-known/advanced place- It's lots much less difficult to start influencing from say, the Caribbean, than it is from a ghetto. This is really because of the truth you're already surrounded with topics that human beings, well, need to appearance. Furthermore, in case you're from a much a good deal less

advanced vicinity, your niches additionally slender down appreciably. For instance, take into account a person from a growing us of a seeking to emerge as a meals influencer. Not very probably to paintings, is it?

These are just a few of the things which can make your begin an awful lot much less complex. This ebook, however, plans to make you an influencer no matter your starting function, so allow's skip over a number of the belongings you'll need to begin being an influencer(except an Instagram account.):

A solid internet connection- Being an influencer revolves during the internet, and despite the fact that you having a strong connection isn't important for importing matters on Instagram, it's miles for various things. For example, you will be reading the opposition in your region of interest, and you want their films to load rapid. You'll additionally regularly have a couple of tabs open while mastering, so its awesome to make certain an brilliant connection.

A virtual digicam- The digital digital digital camera is probably one of the most important topics that an Instagram influencer desires to own. After all, all of your income comes from images. While a few do get away with sincerely their phone virtual digicam, I wouldn't advocate this route, and we'll be searching at some of the first-rate access-level cameras to get later.

Adobe Photoshop/Other enhancing software program- Let's face it, nearly all the content material fabric you word on Instagram has been edited or tampered with in a few way. Putting "nofilter" next to a photo of a model, doesn't without delay advise that she hasn't spent three hours improving her curves to appearance ideal. Even if you aren't a beauty influencer, you'll want to make sure components of your pics pop out and be more high-quality.

While there are unique equipment(specially on-line ones,) that you may use in your career, the ones three are in reality vital so as to even begin. We'll be exploring distinct alternatives, especially on line ones, as they come up.

Now then, allow's expect you're simply broke, how do you begin your Instagram up?

From Zero To Hero

The first element you want is a public library. Most public libraries will provide unfastened internet, or at worst, will provide internet to their members. A club at a public library will normally be hundreds a lot much less pricey than searching for your personal net. You can installation your Instagram account through surely certainly one of their PC's(you may download Android emulators with out price, and paintings off of there.)

Next, you'll want a digital camera. If you have got were given already got a very good cellular telephone, you're on a roll. Otherwise, you'll need to be very extremely good to passers thru manner of at places in that you want to take photographs of what your niche is. These gained't be the awesome brilliant photos, so that you want to make sure that your angling and lighting fixtures are without a doubt stellar.

Finally, if you can't get a licence for enhancing software program software program, you could use loose ones like Gimp.

Once you've commenced getting a strong income, you can invest the proceeds into enhancing your setup.

Now then, what in case you aren't completely broke, but aren't precisely Bill Gates both?

In that case, I although wouldn't propose getting an notable virtual digicam proper now. Don't get me incorrect, an terrific digicam will take your content material material to every different degree, however it does rate a massive amount of cash. You'll want to make sure influencing without a doubt is some aspect you need to do earlier than dipping in.

With that being said, there are cameras which may be underneath $500 that I may endorse to you when you've decided to shop for one:

DSLR- Nikon D3400

The Nikon D3400 is the best camera for you in case you're cause on pursuing the DSLR path. It will permit you to make expert-searching content cloth material at a fragment of the charge of a higher camera. In the arms of an beginner(and it's going to take years till your pictures comes close to to a professional.) It is pretty similar to a excessive-end virtual digicam.

Furthermore, it has awesome ISO control and battery existence. If there's any out of doors paintings in your vicinity of interest, then this digital camera might be best for you. Sure, there are different DSLR cameras with longer battery lives, however most of them are over the double the fee. Video stabilization is a few different exquisite function letting you seize the lifestyles exterior without any troubles.

Mirrorless- Sony a6000

This might be the first-rate non-DSLR virtual virtual digital camera that a sum underneath $500 can purchase. It takes excellent, professional-searching images and has been very surely critiqued for the way nicely it does vegetation and fauna images.

Much similar to the digital digicam earlier than it, this one takes superb, certain images with out breaking the financial institution. A massive downside to mirrorless cameras however, is that the primary lenses have a tendency to be pretty not unusual. The identical is real with the a6000. If you aren't restricting your self to outside pics, you'll battle pretty a piece to get DSLR-degree best out of this virtual camera. One of the high-quality capabilities of this digicam is its Wi-Fi integration, letting you transmit your documents to and from your cellphone with out a hassle.

3

CAPTIVATING YOUR AUDIENCE

G

aining an target audience on Instagram is genuinely the toughest a part of the adventure to turning into an influencer. Because of that, this financial disaster may be split into many sections, committed to ensuring that your Instagram is right enough to capture your audience's interest.

Using The Right Profile Picture

I see influencers, or at the least people seeking to emerge as so, using an beside the point profile picture for their Instagram. If you're a food influencer, you'll need your profile image to have some problem to do with meals.

Our audiences have brief attention spans, in truth, they grow to be shorter by using the usage of the day. You can't waste humans's time with clicking in your profile to find out what it's about, you want to offer it as fast as possible, and that's along with your profile picture.

Make A Bio That Sticks Out

The bio is honestly the most underrated part of the influencer's toolkit. Your bio wants to set up who you are, and more importantly, get your reader to pay hobby.

One of the primary matters that a ability follower will see to your account is your bio, and you want them to take into account it. Not simplest that, you need your bio to be complete of facts, at the same time as being furnished in a swish way.

First off, make certain that your bio includes your niche. If you're a travel blogger, the first or 2nd a part of your bio should be "tour blogger."

This is because of the reality now, when someone searches for "tour blogger" on Instagram, your weblog will pop up.

Another element that's very useful to take a look at is formatting. The Instagram app sucks for this. Make positive which you're offering the data about your self in a graceful and orderly style.

Learn Your Hashtags

Before posting your first positioned up, you'll need to apprehend what hashtags follow to it. These days, they're the principle manner of trying to find content material material material on Instagram. The best manner to discover what hashtags are presently trending on your niche is finding a greater influential influencer and looking at which hashtags they're the use of.

There are techniques of the use of hashtags, one is placing them within the textual content #You Do #It Like #This. I've located that this has a bent to bring about captions which might be more difficult to study, and normally an entire lot more unappealing to readers. The particular, which I've determined works lots higher, is placing all your hashtags on the prevent of your positioned up. This we could the reader leaf through your hashtags at their amusement, in area of being bombarded with bulky blue text.

Write Good Captions

Much like collectively at the side of your bio, there isn't actually a fixed of policies you can simply observe and make your captions proper. This is specially because it relies upon at the niche. You need to understand your target market, as an instance, an investment influencer might in all likelihood genuinely need to write " Bitcoin up 20% #BullMarket" and that might be enough for a informal placed up. On the opposite hand, a higher one could write that, depart off a few empty strains, then skip into an assessment on why it spiked 20%.

Another particular way to make sure your captions are interesting is to make a story to go with your photo. Try to make it non-public, easy to relate to, and remarkable. I'll let you in on a piece mystery right here-it doesn't need to be truely proper.

Look At Your Feed As A Whole

Your feed must virtually no longer seem like a collection of excellently-taken images. Instead, your feed desires to look like a photo in itself. The entire feed desires to study a sample, if in nothing else, then in editing style or shade scheme. You don't need contrasting colorations to be abound at the same time as fans open your feed.

After all, that is Instagram, first impressions are well worth their weight in gold. Make exceptional your feed seems as harmonic as viable.

Don't Post Blurry Photos

Okay positive, this seems apparent, however limitless human beings regardless of the fact that do this. Sure, the portrait placing to your iPhone offers terrific popularity to the object within the front of it, and offers a professional-esque appearance. Here's the detail, it doesn't truely do it in stages like a professional camera does, so the devices out of attention appear like they in reality have emerge as blurry, and that isn't the fantastic look.

Post Consistently

You'll have found that most influencers publish their content material on a daily foundation, a few even more than one times an afternoon. This is because of the reality Instagram's set of regulations closely favors folks who put up constantly, and positioned up often, over people who don't.

If you're essential about turning into an influencer, you want to pick out out a posting time desk and hold on with it. Ideally, this could be at the least every day. Studies have showed that posting regularly results in more target market engagement. Furthermore, Instagram is more likely to recommend your account.

Now, does this advocate you need to take multiple photos every day? Luckily, no it doesn't. There are packages like Buffer, which let you time table your posts. This way you can take the images, write the captions, and the posts might be posted routinely at times you picked.

Use Stories

Similarly to posting constantly, you have to publish every day tales to your feed, simply so your target marketplace can revel in connected and fixed up collectively collectively along with your lifestyles. Furthermore, Instagram's set of guidelines carefully favors individuals who submit stories often.

Stories are extraordinary due to the truth they're an easy way for people to find out you. Because of this, it's remarkable to apply your very last submit or , and submit them as stories too sometimes. Make positive you don't do this too frequently, however, as your modern-day target audience might also additionally start to become bored of seeing the equal photos twice.

Get A Business Account

If you're excessive about influencing as a profession, then you definately definately need an Instagram employer account. This is a wonderful element for influencers, as it offers you get entry to to Instagram Analytics. Instagram Analytics let you see hundreds of data about your fans. You'll benefit get right of entry to to matters starting from age ranges to region. This lets you customize your content cloth in a manner that it every continues your modern-day target marketplace satisfied, and engages with audiences you haven't tapped into sincerely but.

This additionally makes you capable of run classified ads, this is able to boom your profits with the resource of a massive margin.

Now, even when you have a study these varieties of tips, it'll take some time that allows you to get enthusiasts. With that being stated, so long as you keep at it, you'll be racking up enthusiasts right away!

Use Follow For Follow's

If you're familiar with Instagram's facts, you possibly don't forget the comply with for comply with craze of its early days. If no longer, permit me provide an motive of:

Follow for following is a exercise in that you take a look at lots of humans which is probably engaged inner an opening. Afterwards, you'll on commonplace get a 50% or so observe again rate. Those that don't comply with you back, you could honestly unfollow at your enjoyment(or preserve following if you revel in their content fabric.)

An opportunity is calling on the #FollowForFollow hashtag, and picking from there. Aspiring influencers generally use that hashtag very regularly to get a starting influx of fans. Keep in mind that after someone else follows you from a FollowForFollow submit, you're predicted to comply with them all over again. Doing this cultivates a wholesome community for special beginning influencers.

4

KEEPING THEM HOOKED

S

urprisingly sufficient, even while you've were given a massive target audience, it isn't precisely easy to hold them round. Sure, few humans will explicitly unfollow you, however till they're attractive, and actively consuming your content material cloth, they aren't absolutely really worth loads to your customers.

Because of this, you want to make sure which you're not first-class developing your follower take into account, but maintaining your present day-day enthusiasts engaged together along with your content material. In nowadays's international, your sincerely sincerely well worth as an influencer isn't measured in the massive form of fanatics which you have, however as an alternative together with your engagement price.

Your engagement rate is calculated by using manner of taking the style of likes, shares, and feedback in a placed up, and dividing it with the beneficial resource of the variety of lovers you have got were given.

This is a way which advanced due to the reality fake followers, and enthusiasts who don't engage, had been costing businesses coins. For a business enterprise to have a high-quality circulate lower lower back on investment(ROI) from you, you want to be bringing in extra income than they may be paying you for. If you've were given a set of fanatics, however they don't truly engage hundreds with what you put up, then they obtained't be bringing in income to your clients whenever fast.

This is truly exceptional for smaller influencers, as they commonly typically have a tendency to have better engagement costs on common. With this being stated, if you wreck into the hundreds of thousands of fans, no emblem is going to be asking a good buy about engagement costs anymore.

So, with that being stated, here's a few hints on maintaining your fans hooked and appealing together along with your content fabric fabric:

Interact With Them In The Comments

In the give up, your goal market is for your Instagram for you. They need to interact with you as a lot as viable. Now, I'm now not telling you to installation Skype calls with all your fans every three days. However, I am telling you to make sure that you're replying to as many feedback as you may. This we may additionally need in your enthusiasts understand that you care about them, and continues them engaged collectively together with your content.

Share Their Posts

Imagine this: you're sitting together together with your parents in the front of the TV. Your desired movie superstar is creating a grand speech, even as all of the sudden, they issue out some thing you've stated. You'd be leaping for joy maximum in all likelihood. This is how your fanatics feel whenever you percent one in every in their posts. In truth, studies has demonstrated that it's one of the quality techniques to hold your engagement fee up. Now, obviously this doesn't need to be all in their content, however a proportion right right here and there lets in out.

Furthermore, if you're observed via another influencer, you would likely bring a number of their intention marketplace over in your Instagram.

Use Story Stickers

Story stickers are practically a godsend for every influencer searching for to up their engagement rate. There are a few sorts of tale stickers, every accurate for their personal features:

1. Question Sticker- The query sticky label is actually what it says on the tin, you submit a query, your target audience responds. Alternatively, you can host an AMA(Ask Me Anything.) On Instagram memories, this shall we your target market get to apprehend you better, and will increase their interest to your emblem.

2. Voting Sticker- The vote casting decal permits you get a better image of your target market. First of all, there's a trend in which famous influencers use balloting stickers as a manner of residing out their day. Your fans vote on what you want to do and also you do it. It additionally helps your enthusiasts revel in like they have got an input on your day, that is great for engagement.

3. Poll Sticker- The ballot sticky label is lots extra constrained than the voting or question

sticky label, however, it additionally takes masses much less strive. For example, even in case you truly took a image of your espresso mug and wrote "how an awful lot do you want espresso?" It may be sufficient.

Add Your Location To Posts

Adding the place of your posts is reasonably trivial, but you might imagine, how precisely does doing that improve engagement? Well, chiefly, your fans need to narrate to you, let's say you put up a photo out of Yellowstone. Now, each time one in all your attentive fanatics is going to Yellowstone, they'll consider you. Some can also additionally even go to locations you've been to purposefully.

Collaborate With Other Influencers

At first, collabs might also appear like they take subjects far from you. After all, now your enthusiasts also are going to be being attentive to this different character. To the alternative! The actual detail approximately fanatics, in desire to clients, is that there's a close toinfinite quantity of influencers they could look at.

This approach that each you and the influencer you collab with may be getting fans from every different. This is one of the amazing techniques to get into the industry in truth. When searching out collaboration partners, live practical. It's pretty no longer in all likelihood you'll collaborate with Kim Kardashian if you have 100 and fifty fanatics.

Reply To Your DM's

Okay here's the factor, as you develop, you'll find out your self doing this lots much less and lots less. After all, your DM's will in all likelihood be swamped with messages, and it's unrealistic to answer to all of that. On the possibility hand, whilst you're even though growing, that is the exceptional way to hold incredible engagement charges.

Memes

This is probably the approach of growing follower engagement available. Have you determined a meme you decided funny? Just slap it on your feed with a vaguely applicable caption. You'll discover that during this element in time, memes unfold like wildfire. Furthermore, posting memes which is probably clean to narrate to makes your fanatics see you as extra of a person, and make it masses simpler for them to relate to you.

Appearances

Now, this one works better the extra fans you've got. Going locations in which you've have been given a high follower rely(Instagram Analytics will allow you to with this.) This will will let you meet some of your fans, and allows cause them to feel along with you cherish them as humans, in place of without a doubt pretty numerous. Naturally, this is a lot harder to do with a few varieties of influencers(say, a food blogger.) But if you can pull it off, it's a brilliant manner to boom engagement.

Ask Your Followers For Input

This can artwork for quite a extremely good deal any influencer obtainable. Let's say you're a meals influencer, your speciality is reviewing community ingesting places. You can placed out a submit/story

lovers will have interaction with you on that. Good recommendation right here is to take the most favored one or and examine through.

By taking the maximum favored one, you boom the chances that your fans will examine they recommended that. For bonus elements, even as reviewing the restaurant you may go away "counseled via @FollowerName." In the caption. This makes your fans experience like a critical part of what makes your brand tick, and also you continuously need to preserve that feeling.

These are the most relevant procedures of keeping your target market addicted to your content material fabric material, and you'll discover that you get masses more best to new clients thru following them.

Leverage Filters

Since Instagram is a visible-based totally social network, the smooth out characteristic is unsurprisingly one in each of its maximum popular functionalities. After all, filters provide a stylish and terrific look to quite an entire lot every photo. While you could use awesome filters for every positioned up, research suggests that that is instead counterproductive. A file thru the usage of WebDam said that 60% of the producers which might be maximum successful on instagram use the identical clean out on every put up.

This achievement has been defined thru noticing that followers opt for influencers with a visual identity. Using terrific filters on each publish makes your feed seem chaotic and untidy. Meanwhile, using the equal one on all your posts shows a experience of identity.

It's even though an extremely good concept to attempt out as many filters as viable, but you must possibly pick only a few of them to use. If you pick to use more than one filter out, make sure that they supplement each super visually.

If you don't want to spend too much time choosing a smooth out to apply, just use Clarendon. It's thru a long way the maximum well-known clear out on Instagram for appropriate purpose. It makes colorful colorings pop out and offers quite a piece of brightness to the snap shots.

On the opposite aspect of the fence, if you aren't an entire lot of keen at the filters that Instagram gives you, you may constantly use filters supplied via a 3rd party software program software and add them on Instagram. You may additionally moreover even edit your private photographs in a software like Photoshop if that's what you're eager on.

Mentions

Mentions are similar to non-consensual collaborations. By bringing up a person on your caption or tale, it permits their lovers to look your positioned up. This expands your accumulate, and the other person doesn't need to be an influencer or some element. Even in case you actually factor out your friend from high school, you'll likely get their fanatics to comply with you. Alternatively, mentioning a brand might also get their interest, or it'd get a number of that emblem's enthusiasts to look at you as nicely.

If you're the use of a emblem's product for your posts, it's a top notch idea to say them now not best because of the motives referred to above, however furthermore because of the reality potential clients will anticipate you've partnered with them. This gives the image of you being professional beyond what's definitely the case, which you can then leverage in negotiations.

Post Videos

Current predictions posted with the aid of Zenith predict that people may be spending 80 four mins in their day searching movies at the net. Even in recent times, the parent sits excessive at sixty seven mins an afternoon. This is a true proverbial goldmine, as many influencers placed up few movies because of them taking more strive on average than pictures do.

If you're not leveraging videos in amassing and maintaining enthusiasts, you're very a bargain missing out. The standard overall performance and recognition of video content material fabric material on Instagram makes it one of the simplest methods to skyrocket your engagement charge.

Think about it, humans are much more likely to have interaction with something the more time they spend on it. Which do you spend greater time searching at, a video or a despite the reality that picture? This makes movement pictures loads much more likely to garner hobby, similarly to likes, remarks, and stocks. Shares are specially essential, because it we could human beings that aren't privy to you be conscious your content cloth less complex.

Instagram already gives plenty of video options that you can use as an influencer. Putting out a stay video is also an brilliant way to engage together with your target market. Q & A periods are pleasant hosted like this, and that they allow your followers not simplest engage with you, but additionally find out greater facts about the influencer they comply with. It's also great for selling your customers' objects and offerings.

Alternatively, you can use pre-recorded content material for hundreds of abilties. You can use it as a regular positioned up, without a doubt growing a announcement. You can use it as a promotional piece for your self, or maybe a promotional piece for your customers.

5

DO I LEAVE MY JOB?

T

his bankruptcy is dedicated to a question that all new influencers ask themselves at a nice time "Is it time to head away my approach but?" Usually, the answer to this query is not any. I even have visible an extended way too many influencers fall into the entice of incomes what resembles a modest income and leaving their undertaking for it, best to move back lower back a month or later.

It's essential to be practical in phrases of this. In this chapter, we'll furthermore don't forget underage influencers who even though don't work, and whether or not or now not they have to get a challenge in the first location. While most of the chapters right here are quite effective in tone, this one is a truth check. You can't find the money for to make a screw up at the same time as leaving your technique, particularly if you have a circle of relatives.

First, allow's get the lots much less complex don't forget out of the way, if you're not an underage influencer you can pass this segment.

I'm Underage/In College, Do I Get A Job?

There are quite some influencers which make it earlier than even being given the chance to start a "regular" career route. Whether in college or possibly earlier than, it's pretty clean to expect that influencing can be your career course for existence, however, even if you're on the younger detail of things, you continue to need to stay realistic.

Consider Your Niche

A lot of college influencers make university-related Instagrams. Whether this is from a personal faculty like Harvard, or your remarkable ol' community university, your region of interest is rooted in your location in lifestyles. You need to invite your self-what takes location as soon as I depart college?

This applies to special age-associated niches as properly. If your entire gimmick is being more youthful to your location of interest, what's your plan for on the same time as you no longer are?

Now, in case your area of interest is clearly tied to how vintage you are, you may want to start each other Instagram which isn't quite as restricted. Alternatively, you've got were given were given 3 options.

1. Give up influencing- This is always a valid preference, in case you're making pretty some cash off being an influencer, you might never need to do it over again. Alternatively, in case you're feeling burnout, it's quality to end at the same time as you're ahead as opposed to have a disappointing, slowly receding profession.

2. Shift your selling factor- This is the selection most young influencers which may be aware of their state of affairs. Say, in case you had a "university" weblog, in which you took snap shots of your campus, buddies, well-known university lifestyles. You should slowly transfer it to a lifestyle Instagram rather. This lets you

stay relevant, and is near sufficient in your unique area of hobby that your target market acquired't phrase you transferring your location of interest. This route does have its dangers although.. Do this too unexpectedly, and your target market may moreover revel in alienated from you. On the opportunity hand, in case you're too slow at the uptake, you'll likely begin too late.

three. Keep on like now not some thing occurred- I've visible this paintings a pair instances. Youth themed feeds which have stayed on-component lengthy after the owner themselves grew out of it. Let's use the university example yet again. As extended as you faux you're in college, your fanatics received't have the ability to tell the distinction, now will they? The trouble with this approach is that it is unpredictable and in no way lasts all the time. After a while, humans will start questioning why a middle-elderly individual is posting approximately college. You also can get uncovered as a fraud at any factor, so I wouldn't recommend it.

Now that we've lengthy past through the ones, I'll keep with the belief which you're slowly switching your vicinity of interest to something greater appropriate. If that's going nicely, we will move onto the red meat of the query, ought to you get a challenge?

Let's have a look at this rationally:

Income

Which is larger, the profits you're making influencing in a mean month, or a interest you can fairly get? Sure, at t is aspect you're despite the fact that probably residing together along with your mother and father(if you're no longer, and influencing is taking you that a long way, you don't want a mission.) But getting to grips with the fee of cash faster instead of later is a wonderful element.

Now, personally I may most effective endorse you no longer get a activity if influencing is earning as a minimum the same amount as a earnings might. This is specially because of the truth influencing isn't very sturdy at that quantity of earnings. You need to find out your self with out an earnings within each week, and none can be the wiser.

Time

Similarly to earlier than, that is taking up greater of some time, influencing or doing a hobby? By this I don't advocate honestly the time that it takes you to publish pix, I imply all the time you spend reading improving and so on. At this age, you need to spend it gradual as it need to be, generally on studying.

Here, influencing will regularly have the threshold, and if so I need to suggest virtually pursuing it with as an awful lot strive as you've been putting in so far.

What If I'm An Adult Looking To Quit Their Job?

If you're an grownup, things get plenty greater complicated. You may additionally have youngsters to attend to, debts to repay, wouldn't it commonly be higher to experience the steadiness of a 9-five pastime?

Not constantly. After all, beyond a wonderful problem, I'd argue influencing is a good deal extra strong than a 9-5. You can get fired from a nine-5 at any point, however an influencer with masses of loads of fans isn't truely going to disappear in a unmarried day despite the truth that they've been in a scandal(see James Charles.) With that being said, right here's a few hints if this is the street you're looking to stroll:

Save At Least three Month's Worth Of Wages

One element you want to maintain in mind before quitting your procedure to pursue influencing is your monetary financial savings. I could endorse having at the least 3 month's well worth of wages in monetary financial savings in advance than diving in. After all, in case your influencing earnings is going stomach up, you'll be unemployed, and the longer the time among your current-day interest and that element, the greater difficult it'll be to get some other activity.

Make Sure You Aren't Relying On Your 9-five Income

So a protracted way, you've been residing collectively together with your influencing profits and your nine-five operating together. By quitting your day task, you'll be reducing your rate variety. Now, in case you're earning enough that a month's wages flow into financial savings every month, you may pull this off effects.

On the alternative hand, in case you're relying on your lovers to increase because you're installing extra try, you is probably in for a impolite awakening. It takes time for Instagram's set of regulations to get yourself up to speed collectively with your new conduct, and it's now not probably you'll get one hundred 000 new fanatics in per week certainly because of the fact you committed more time.

Be Ready For It To Be Less Fun

The second some issue becomes a profession, in choice to some element you do best for amusing, it receives a positive amount of satisfaction taken out of it. This is kind of high high-quality to expose as a great deal as you too, influencing certainly received't be as amusing because it modified into before. That's now not pronouncing there acquired't be moments you'll experience, however at that component it's not your thing hustle, it's your undertaking. That approach treating it as a interest, walking each day, and making sure you're doing the entirety for your energy to up that follower recollect.

6

THE KINDS OF INFLUENCERS

Y

ou shouldn't be amazed to discover that there are notable types of influencers, every with their very very own specialists and cons. First off, allow's begin with the handiest all of us preserve in thoughts even as a person says the word influencer:

Mega Influencers

HYPR Brands' CEO has described mega influencers to be those which can be:

"...extra famous than influential. They aren't always mission rely professionals, however they definitely offer loads of accumulate in a single hit."

These are human beings like, say, Kim Kardashian or Kylie Jenner. These influencers have fans a long way eclipsing the determine of a million. They can control to pay for to charge massive costs to their customers, due to the reality they're properly properly worth it.

You'll word that maximum of these influencers have quite low engagement charges, in any case, no longer all of Kylie Jenner's images have over 10 million likes, heck, a few don't even destroy via the 5 million decide. Despite her having 138 million fans to this point. On the alternative hand, this doesn't actually...depend even as you've had been given get entry to to an goal marketplace of 138 million people.

This shape of influencer will often art work with principal producers like Gucci or Apple with a view to sell their products. It's not that uncommon for mega influencers to charge over $500 000 for a unmarried promotional positioned up. After all, they're attaining out to tens of tens of tens of hundreds of thousands of human beings. It's pretty hard to position a rate on that.

With that being said, there are a pair issues with those, the primary being the big fee. Smaller or medium sized groups clearly cannot offer you with the cash for this form of promotion. The 2d is the lack of personalization, getting an ad with a mega influencer is similar to taking walks a business on TV. Sure, a number of people will see it, however how many turns into your customers?

In any case, if you belong to this class, you don't need me to tell you your earning capability.

Macro Influencers

Now, macro influencers are quite much like their mega opposite numbers, besides they have a propensity to be net celebrities. Usually, the ones aren't quite family names, however all of us that's familiar with their issue remember wide variety may be proper here.

To provide an instance, permit's take Consoleskins. They got their recognition with the aid of doing one clean trouble- making splendor adjustments to gaming system.

Usually, the ones influencers can also have over 2 hundred 000 fans, however furthermore typically cap out at a few million.

The gain that macro influencers have over mega influencers is that they clearly have a niche. For instance, if you placed an advert on Kylie Jenner, all and sundry and their mother goes to appearance that. On the other hand, if you use an Instagram like, say @Consoleskins, you're handiest going to advantage humans which might be actually into online game device skins.

A downside is that, properly, they however value pretty plenty. Furthermore, despite the reality that they come up with reach in a gap, frequently that vicinity of hobby can be a piece too large for the brand's capabilities.

These influencers are wildcards in phrases of follower engagement prices, as a few have colourful communities even as others are content material with without a doubt a bigger follower depend.

Their charges additionally variety wildly, so you might also moreover find out a few doing commercials for as little as some thousand bucks, even as others want a far large share of a companies earnings. If you belong in this elegance, ensuring to maximise your outreach, similarly to follower engagement fees.

Micro Influencers

Micro influencers are people who have amongst 10 000 and one hundred 000 lovers. Their Instagram feeds tend to be especially specialised, and that is why producers price them. They are typically professionals at their hassle take into account, and all in their enthusiasts are clearly engrossed in what they're posting about.

Micro influencers have a tendency to have quite immoderate engagement fees, or at the least, they want immoderate engagement costs at the manner to look like precious belongings to a brand.

These influencers regularly have a quite personal relationship with their fans, which leads to their fans trusting them masses greater than they might a macro or mega influencer. A micro influencer is extra corresponding to a close-by celebrity than they may be a international movie star much like the mega influencer. This way that at the identical time as they've a small following, that small following belongs to a strict area of interest and that's exactly what brands are searching out.

These influencers are frequently hired thru small and medium organizations. While they don't have quite the cash to hire a macro or mega influencer, they recognise precisely which goal market they need to hook up with.

When it involves incomes ability, the most vital detail is to ensure that you're developing your following, and that your engagement fees are excessive. Besides this, ensure you've have been given a strict vicinity of hobby(a sushi Instagram gets lots extra attention from clients than a popular meals one.) You need to be looking at rate tags between $250 and $one thousand relying on follower be counted and engagement.

Chapter 7: Approach To Successful Influencing

Influencing is hastily turning into the most desired abilities via way of todays leaders. The requirement to assist people are available in the course of the way of believing is a have to as organizations and industries constantly alternate assembly the necessities of the economic weather and the requirement to maintain costs.

Influencing can be described as' The energy or capability of factors or people to come to be a compelling pressure on or create impacts on the sports, conduct, views, and so forth. Of others'.

Influencing is an technique in which you have an effect on the mind and behaviors of someone else and take them spherical on your manner of questioning. Unlike Negotiation, in that you try to be a part of up with the man or woman in the center, influencing brings the character for your degree.

Influencing is probably carried out on a large form of instances - Trying to shop for a ultra-cutting-edge approach or insurance exceeded with the Board of Directors, helping a patron to have a examine the gain of a product, assisting group of workers to decide that change is essential. Essentially, a massive range of things.

A excellent influencer is ready to:

Indicate the benefits of their thoughts

Neutralize resistance earlier

Find opportunity strategies to have an impact on others

Listen attentively to what others say

Uncover want and desires

Empathize continuously

See how others respond

Develop and hold rapport throughout

Eliminate inadequate statements from their language

Rehearse, rehearse, rehearse.

The outcomes of the influencing improvement are: Total Commitment - i.E. Great concept, want I should think about it. At what time can we begin?

Overall Agreement - Not a terrible idea I surely have have been given or two doubts

Compliance - Ok, you're the boss. I anticipate we might better start

Wide-open war of words - This will no longer paintings and right here is why Hidden sabotage - (Thinks) you reckon it's going to paintings; I will show you incorrect.

When influencing, we're searching out reaction number one, or huge range .

To Influence nicely, you may use an clean five step approach. The measures are:

1. Build Rapport - Use the records you have got were given approximately the character to growth a connection and engage with the character.

2. Questions - Attempt to take a look at the person's present day stance approximately the

scenario and don't forget in which any objections can come via.

3. Listen - Actively experience the responses the person has furnished you, and display which you are listening.

4. Benefits - Sell the benefits of the belief of yours on the individual. Wherever feasible, relate them to the strategies that you acquire thru the individual. Constantly have evidence to decrease again up the benefits of yours.

5. Decision - Push for a preference. Try and in no manner permit them to vanish and endure in mind it. Do not ask them to disappear and' query the boss' - you need to ask to speak with the supervisor.

The thriller to effective influencing is steering.

Using the 5-step machine, you could do the training. Think approximately what you are planning to do at each one of the levels.

You can use an Influencing Plan to assist with the practise. In order to layout your concept stand out, you need to remember how you are probable to border your idea. You should:

Engage the audience - What are the advantages of your concept?

What distinction can it create?

Inform - What's the prevailing scenario? So why do topics have to alternate? What proof do you've got?

Explain - Just what does the device are like? How need to you placed it into movement?

Project - What'll subjects be like thru following the concept?

Once another time, the schooling plan possesses a template to assist with this.

We nearly honestly all need to find out how you can have an effect on others. Obviously, it's going to probably be top notch in case we will virtually make humans decide to what we endorse, and offer in to what we would like and feature the capacity to make topics a great deal less complicated - from your career to relationships and in organisation.

Learning the manner to persuade others also can get you extra friends and growth suitable relationships, and being prepared to short attain your desires and dreams in existence. To have the capability to persuade and persuade, the subsequent are a few important matters that you have to recall.

Understand your self.

For positive you have got got your non-public personal strengths and weaknesses. You have the capability to apprehend yourself and look at what is blocking off you to be any person who may also want to outcomes convince or effect others is however one step that is essential, to begin with. Successful human beings recognize themselves lots this is why they're capable to plan nicely and therefore can gain their desires quick.

Hone listening capabilities.

Good listening is a crucial a part of top communique - it is a important device in being geared up to persuade and persuade human beings. Learn to hone your listening competencies by way of way of giving humans your complete hobby and a actual hobby within the goals of others.

One method which is regularly-applied in influencing others is understanding their want and desires and assists them to artwork on it or fulfill it. Having the ability to cope with the needs of others is one manner to encourage them to comply with.

Focus on becoming likable.

Learning the manner to persuade others starts offevolved offevolved from making humans which consist of you. To be equipped to perform this, you've got to reveal them your actual hobby and be a person who offers out accurate electricity to others.

Be best and assist make the human beings genuinely experience they may be vital. Learn the manner to care, appreciate and praise clearly additionally and give your whole hobby to them. When you would like to recognize how you may have an impact on them, you want to offer first earlier than you could gather.

Supply criticisms with treatment.

Another critical issue you need to take be aware in finding out the manner to have an effect on others and persuade them to bear in mind the approach you do is giving careful criticisms. If you criticize, you are sincerely influencing others to move your way or change their behavior or beliefs.

Nevertheless, it is essential which you criticize nicely with out driving them out. Hurting human beings is surely a few element that could will will let you be unlikable. Don't criticize human beings, as an alternative, criticize the motion.

You may additionally need to start with criticizing your errors earlier than you offer criticisms to others and discover the manner to provide superb criticisms. This way, you could impact their wondering without dropping rapport.

Be assured and talk with any luck. You possibly might not be privy to the numerous' ummms' you have on your conversations but those might also provide the goal market a touch of doubt and uncertainty.

If you allow doubt to enter into their minds, it would additionally cause them to uncertain approximately following you. Find out how to speak right away and exude trust that makes humans want to test and believe.

Begin with those basics in locating out how to influence people and you may in all likelihood have a awesome begin in influencing and persuading others to do everything you would love them to do.

Chapter 8: The Psychology Of Influence

Have you struggled to show capability customers into raving fans? Or do you work with humans however war to provide the cease end cease end result which you need? In that case, spare a minute or to reflect onconsideration on the psychology of effect as it's far a problem that can be mastered and perfected.

The psychology of have an effect on covers the 6 widespread thoughts as follows:

RECIPROCITY

You want to first, take some time to get preserve of it once more. Just what does this suggest? All parents realise that people get from human beings. And humans will be predisposed to be greater prepared to go together with what you are asking of them - whether or not or now not or no longer it's Liking your Facebook page, commenting to your blog, and providing you with their electronic mail cope with - when you have furnished them something to start with.

That is why' ethical bribes' are applied in on line advertising and marketing, by way of using way of imparting leads a bit of useful data or record to induce them to expose their e mail deal with. It is also the motive free samples are done in offline marketing - that is the psychology of have an effect on working at its first-rate.

CONSISTENCY OF COMMITMENT

When humans devote themselves to a suggestion or idea, both verbally or in writing, there is a substantially more chance that they will honor that commitment If they experience that idea or concept is congruent with their self-image.

So how are you going to get them to think that?

A perfect on-line instance is with the aid of the use of using a survey - when individuals have replied to your survey via offering you their opinion, they'll be extra organized to take part on your resultant schooling or electronic mail advertising and advertising and advertising and marketing and marketing.

Just making a little exchange of phase is capable of make a big difference. Thus, rather than walking order as "If you convert the plans of yours, please name us", rephrased to tactfully request

"Will you kindly contact us in case your plans change?" - led to an huge drop off in no shows for a eating place thinking about the fact that diners had verbally devoted to calling whether or not or not or now not they exchange their plans. Simply don't forget the manner you could follow this to the internet global.

Furthermore, even as any individual has already been devoted to shopping for a hassle from you, then use the very terrific moment to provide them some trouble special to shop for, and offer an upsell, takes place when they presently have their credit score score score card thru - making your thanks internet internet web page the very terrific on line real property you can have and the very nice risk to apply of the psychology of effect to your gain.

Personal PROOF

Everyone is normally scared to create a choice that could lead them to appearance absurd, but in case they see others have created the identical choice or taken the identical motion, they may be greater prepared to act!

That is exactly why, of route, real critiques are very effective, as people are plenty extra willing do subjects in case they word specific humans speaking about it having performed it, and acquired plenty from it.

It is unusual to apprehend, no matter the fact that people will don't forget the testomony of any stranger or a third birthday celebration man or woman earlier than they may accept as actual with the genuine birthday celebration character promoting the object or presenting the facts! Unusual, but actual!

AUTHORITY

Individuals are extra prepared to check from or take note of those with related facts or authority.

In elegant, pleasant the smooth symbols of authority is able to make humans reply proper now - along with titles, qualifications, authentic clothing or commercial enterprise suits - but the ones bodily symbols are tough to reveal on line.

And so a exquisite method of installing authority at the internet is thru walking a blog, and getting many comments to your weblog posts. Or absolutely preserving your self out as an expert is going some of techniques additionally.

In order to be a seasoned, you essentially need to be one soar ahead, or e one idea ahead, of your opportunities - you do no longer need to turn out to be an Emeritus Professor prepared in the psychology of impact, or in your problem of choice to have the capability to impart recommendation or records.

LIKING/FRIENDSHIP

I talked about previously that individuals get from humans, however permit me to qualify that similarly, really due to the truth humans buy from folks that they apprehend and like. This is some of the pillars of appeal marketing and marketing and advertising (link to video) or connection advertising and marketing and advertising and advertising and advertising.

That is the reason it's miles important to speak to people in your list like they had been your buddy - so company language or corporate-talk will no longer paintings! , it technique that a few humans will unsubscribe out of your list if they decide that they do not which includes you - however that is great - they possibly did now not have an affinity for you.

Video Clip is a nice hearth method of conveying your character; supporting individuals to installation you're likable, same with an powerful tool in establishing friendships with your prospects or followers. By manner of video, you could appeal to folks that are just like you and who proportion your outlook and values in life.

SCARCITY

Individuals do not like missing out on a excellent deal!

What is extra, , they want what they can't have!

Perceived scarcity, rarity, or diminishing availability can create name for. Sometimes without a doubt saying "When they're lengthy long gone, they're lengthy long gone!" might be up to scratch.

Qualifying who a product or training is for makes human beings choice to have that qualifying organisation!

Stating that you will discover genuinely twenty downloadable answers will not reduce the mustard, however - the dearth need to be real and actual.

If you use those concepts ethically in a non-manipulative way, then your have an impact on of persuasion may be longer-lasting and powerful. Your goal is producing so many raving fanatics as humanly viable

Adding the above-noted ideas in and information the psychology of impact and why individuals purchase, will assure yours as a web marketer.

Chapter 9: Why The Influencer Should Be Your New Best Friend

Social networking is the modern day first rate motor powering phrase of mouth and, as we understand, phrase of mouth may be the quickest technique to distribute the gospel of your emblem.

We've determined that in every effort to gather successful word of mouth advertising and advertising, you have were given attained the don't forget and dedication of leaders inside the market and of the consumer groups. These leaders will observe your product first and, in case they'll be satisfied, inform all people just how first-rate it's miles.

An influencer is all people who is commonly called an expert with regards to your organisation. They recognize what groups they'll be specializing in, they recognize what gadgets are first rate and which ones aren't.

The most massive component you need to look at an influencer is that they have got a voice this is relied on with the useful resource of their friends and that includes an possibility for you and your organization.

Precisely why Is the Influencer Important?

There are many elements why you desire these influencers on your group. They'll assist electricity the word-of-mouth advertising and marketing marketing campaign of yours on Social networking. People will ask them what they undergo in thoughts approximately your new product and they'll consider what they are saying more than they will without a doubt trust an commercial.

After they supply their opinion on your services or products, that is what all their pals, enthusiasts, and readers will accept as true with. Think of these human beings as being an extension in your emblem. In case they may be satisfied than an entire lot of their fans are thrilled, if they may be reputation in location for you, so are their fans.

Something to undergo in mind is the reality that everyone of your clients is usually a strong influencer. Shop round on commercial enterprise business employer blogs, Facebook pages, and Twitter profiles to find out the people who are talking often and loudly. Search for patron evaluation blogs which can be loaded with net web site site visitors and in comments.

How can I attain them?

When you understand a number of the key influencers you desire to link them to your company is the least invasive way possible. You can do this thru on almost all Social networking channels thru connecting to them, tagging, re-tweeting, and so on.

You can touch upon the records the located up and in locations you are conscious that they'll be reading. If your agency shows them appreciate as a extraordinary voice within the marketplace, they will begin spreading the superb phrase approximately your brand.

Influencers fall someplace amongst traditional media shops and superstar. They pass over the issues of monetizing on a channel in which they have advanced a real following. For durability, realistic influencers experience they should stay real to their goal market and private emblem. There aren't any advertising and marketing recommendations, no set fees and the functioning parameters range for every body.

So if beginning an influencer plan (paid or no longer), it's miles important to reflect onconsideration on wherein and the way your brand have to have up.

As a logo, a splendid way to accumulate the maximum out of coping with influencers is with the aid of growing encounters for them. Influencers are continuously looking for possibilities to create content material material and percentage facts of their day.

Tarte Cosmetics uses influencers on journeys to a lovable, superb vicinity more than one times each 12 months to set up a product launch (#trippinwithtarte). Additional profitable makes supply influencers on sourcing behind-the-scenes excursions or journeys of their head office or e manufacturing, or they definitely allow influencers on a private preserve excursion.

Personalization is critical. Influencers love sharing reviews which is probably created in particular for his or her character. Influencers have shared their testimonies in the Lab extensively on their social channels, absolutely which include Bite's name on the chart.

You can personalize additives of your emblem on the same time as liaising with influencers. Unique ship sports and outs with custom provides are a few examples of this.

Trends are exquisite. If your emblem is capable of leap on a trouble that is trending and make a product or statistics regular with that path, you're much more likely to look extra coverage.

Unicorns are well-known inside the make-up network inside the meanwhile, whilst athleisure is one aspect hundreds of apparel makes have been capitalizing on for some time. Of course, remaining in trends and being reactive is vital.

Conflicts are thrilling. Launching a product or beginning on a marketing campaign? Consider virtually how influencers can encompass their voice via way of a mission it's miles fun for them to attract hobby in your commercial enterprise emblem.

Challenges are a laugh, smooth to have a look at and allow influencers to have interaction with every distinctive. Profitable demanding situations encompass the bean boozled mission which set in movement with Harry Potter's flavored jelly beans, ice bucket undertaking which raised lots and hundreds for ALS and the Disney assignment which draws pretty a few awareness on the producer.

Engage with them. Commenting and liking on influencers posts is very essential as a brand and allows preserve the connection intact. This will help to maintain your logo on the top-of-mind as managing influencers can go along with the go together with the flow and ebb, consequently maintaining that regular touchpoint is crucial to non-forestall achievement.

Overall, it's miles crucial you operate influencers which might be captivated with your brand, or as a minimum keen to investigate more. With any influencer, it's vital to recollect no longer nice their lovers however feedback and engagement on the data they produce.

Chapter 10: How Can You Recognize Influencers?

Some people might be extra aware of influencers of their organization or area of interest than others. Nevertheless, it's far essential to understand that influencers are a rather critical part of your expert success.

It calls for a good buy of exertions to obtain influencer kingdom and it is really beneficial to surround your self with influencers who will will can help you decorate your agency on the following health diploma.

Capturing the hobby of different human beings on line

There isn't always any doubt that your content cloth is pinnacle-shelf. Nevertheless, it is no longer usually sufficient. You do not want to constantly create content material that speaks to at least one-of-a-kind people in a profound manner irrespective of the reality that you want to get extraordinary humans to marketplace your content material and to talk approximately it. In a nutshell, you require influencers to advise and manual what you are giving.

Suppose an influencer proportion your content material, it's far going to transport a pretty long manner in your capacity to raise your articles. The wonderful element about influencers isn't only that the man or woman has a exceptional quantity of trustworthiness and credibility, however you'll be assured that the man or woman works very tough to maintain his function as an influencer.

The identical as in any place of power, if the influencer does not paintings tough to hold his influencer popularity, that man or woman might not be recognized as an influencer all the time.

The problems of selecting the correct influencers

With regards to figuring out influencers, you want to be discerning. Some influencers are a excellent fit for the ones enterprise businesses and all commercial agency humans. It truly relies upon to your brand and what you are trying to carry out alongside facet your company.

When you have got accumulated a precis of functionality influencers, you need to check each one thoroughly and keep in mind if each one will benefit your business and beautify what you are trying to perform.

You need to make sure that your very last listing of influencers isn't always lengthy. Those influencers that make your very last reduce are individuals who'll allow you to take your industrial business enterprise to the following fitness degree.

The fantastic aspect of influencers is the reality that they normally recognize extraordinary influencers which is probably terrific and in the event that they charge your approach and the content cloth, they may be more than pleased to share. At this juncture, you are most probable wondering the way you could pick out out your influencers within the exceptional manner possible.

Start out via figuring out which influencer you need to have a look at and begin to observe them continuously: You'll find out net techniques which can be supplied to will will let you apprehend the very amazing influencers for

you. You want to look for individuals who've an first rate on line presence and who market compelling concerns via their writing.

The first advantage you want with the resource of performing that is you may not genuinely live associated with the influencer but to anyone else to who that influencer is hooked up. That's a extremely good and powerful technique to widen your sphere of effect and to begin to decorate your recognition and boom your publicity.

The dating ought to be mutual:

Relationships, are claimed to be mutual through the usage of using nature. You will find out an entire lot of techniques in which you could assist every other. In many instances, coins in no way changes arms. You have a few component beneficial (a product or a business enterprise) that a person needs and requires and every other person has something it's miles treasured for you too.

You deliver to every different and, with a bit of luck, you could each be happy ultimately. In the occasion that it comes in your interactions and dating at the facet of your influencer, it'd flawlessly be a courting that doesn't incorporate the identical mind-set which you have if you meet up with others.

When you have created a connection with that unique influencer, if you every paintings with that connection, there can be no accurate reason why it can't be considered a protracted-lasting one. It's clearly crucial that your influencer and yourself join on numerous stages. Get to understand one another as individuals. A robust base of get hold of as true with is going to be the final consequences of it.

Influence and access aren't one and the same:

At this level, it is important to hold in thoughts that deciding on quantity over outstanding is maximum in all likelihood now not a smart choice. Having the capability to mention you have 500+ connections is probably thoughts-blowing to loads of human beings but how a

113

variety of the ones 500+ humans do you actually communicate with mechanically?

Most in all likelihood now not a large percentage of them, accurate?

It will make plenty more revel in to pick out outstanding over amount. It's a wise selection to discriminate as regards to the human beings you permit into your circle. You would like to get the first-rate out of those interactions in the long run.

Influencers are a completely crucial part of your corporation. Nevertheless, you need to pick out your influencers sensibly so that the relationship you percentage with the opportunity character can be the excellent that it is able to be. You need it to have quality, together beneficial outcomes.

When you have got created a dating with considered one of your influencers, you may consider in that individual to paintings his magic as regards to revel in in that particular location of hobby. You can take it clean and benefit the blessings of that knowledge.

If you're aware about it or now not, via the use of selecting out the most suitable influencer, you are selecting out the maximum suitable character to precise your story to, and so that you can resonate with a number of different people.

Chapter 11: The Best Way To Be An Influencer In Your Industry

Undoubtedly you have got got heard the phrase, influencer" from numerous parents within the business enterprise. You have probably assumed that now not truly are influencers vital and you've concluded that clearly turning into an influencer is a few problem that allows you to will will let you bring your organization to the next diploma.

There exist lots of numerous elements about why influencers are vital for you professionally. Influencers convey credibility beyond the belief you have got were given created for your commercial business enterprise.

You are maximum likely glad that influencers are vital to your commercial enterprise employer. Nevertheless, nowadays it's time you recognize why you need to come to be an influencer and clearly how you are set about making that display up.

At this degree, you're maximum possibly wondering you strive turning into an influencer. Effectively, you could find out some definitive measures you may look at for getting there. Nevertheless, it's miles essential with a view to apprehend at this particular juncture that it might not display up in a unmarried day. It goes to take a chunk on the same time as and try in an effort to get to be the influencer which you would love to be.

Accept the concept of influencer:

An influencer is an character that has a bargain of credibility with him. The person has a simply useful effect on the place of hobby and your logo. Influencers furthermore characteristic fans.

Followers are to be had in lots of forms, like those who regularly examine blogs, the influencer has shared or human beings who've interaction regularly with that influencer. At the same time, influencers can to be had in precise patterns and sizes. The hassle that every influencer have in commonplace is the reality that they've the capability to have an effect on distinct people.

In one in all a kind phrases, they are quite great individuals and so they should not be overlooked as some element short of that. Influencers have a presence and their phrase consists of weight. You can consider them as authority figures.

They are the gold modern day in that you want to base your commercial enterprise corporation method. The truth is you are not the most effective man or woman who recognizes the fee of influencers. Others realise and embrace their fee likewise.

Focus in your location of hobby: As you begin to take measures to be an influencer, the number one trouble you need to perform is identifying in that you would love your have an impact without delay to live. The decision is going to be based mostly on wherein your passions lie. Should you choose to be an influencer in a location which does now not virtually contact you deeply, you may not have the functionality to drag it off.

When you haven't been prepared to influence yourself of your ardour and willpower, precisely how are you going to expect exclusive individuals to be satisfied of your respective willpower and ardour. It's really that easy. Nevertheless, it is honestly critical you are at once related together along with your location of hobby just so others can join you with that region of hobby too. In fact, it truely is a important a part of your branding. You need to keep away from talking approximately severa topics. You want to be related together together with your place of hobby. Or else, your influencer reputation is going to be diluted and you could no longer be perceived a PRO for a few factor.

Try giving others the benefit of your records: The fact is it's some element being experienced (even going up to now as to end up an expert on your area of hobby) although it's a further element honestly (and masses greater of a present) to have the potential to train any other man or woman what you recognize just so a person can broaden expertise on it. What you could reap is a real take a look at of your influencer recognition.

In this precise context (with all the net interactions which you want in your enterprise), the super (and maximum probably the best) technique to try to do that by means of way of disclosing articles (in whichever shape(s) you want to talk about. A super manner to perform that is via posting blogs, newsletters, films, and so on.

Another notable manner to talk about expertise is thru internet discussions which can be compelling and applicable to others. Remember to be aware about your social media profiles in any respect time. You do now not want them to become static.

You need to decorate your recognition on the distinct social networking profiles and keep parents for your social circles near you so that you can boom your relationships with them.

Offer your opinion to other human beings: Everyone loves to recognize that your critiques and their emotions do not forget. As an influencer, it's miles loads greater vital for you and in your organization. There is simply no longer whatever like a silent influencer. It's a contradicting. The more you have interaction human beings, the more they may be inclined to find out who you're and the entirety you recognize.

Both of those are important in your persisted success. It's extensively less despite the fact that you are probably to be twisting their arm even as it is about getting them to take part with you. They will constantly be willing, furnished that the interactions advantage their interest.

You truly want to make certain this is the case. An influencer, need to be prepared to gather that resultseasily. Even in case you are yet to be an influencer, this method goes to serve you correctly.

System up till you drop:

Networking has constantly been and might often be an immensely crucial element of the commercial enterprise employer operation. The possible procedures in which you could network are each online or offline.

Needless to say, it does now not want one or the opposite man or woman. You can network in every manner. Only you could determine which method works ideal in your unique business company.

At the center of networking achievement may be the relationships themselves. The fact is that now not absolutely everyone have to (or will) take time to wait networking sports that's why you need to be flexible to

obtain success with the opposite person. When you community frequently with people, they may get to discover who you're and they'll start to do not forget in you, discover you proper, and you may be at the pinnacle of their thoughts each time they want what you're supplying.

Recognize the engagement blessings

Engage your audience can be very essential for you for without it, you will be without a doubt stopped to your tracks. Nevertheless, you have the capability to prevent that from going on.

With the entirety you need to provide, whether or now not you are an influencer probable or you're at the manner to getting an influencer, numerous people might want to be near you to bask inside the glory of all which you need to offer.

Influencers are especially essential within the seasoned region and sure it's far going to be actually nicely well worth the time and effort that you want to positioned into it to be an influencer your self. Individuals will recognize what you've got were given to say and they may use you for the solutions they do not really revel in they may be capable of expand themselves.

Ensure you are making your influencer interactions an vital element of your social media advertising and marketing technique. It need to be some of the constructing blocks of your enterprise' foundation.

You will keep a place of esteem in your business enterprise and social businesses will gain from all of the hard art work. The influencer reputation of yours will appeal to people and feature them coming and you in a worldwide in which it's far greater complicated than ever to capture high-quality humans's interest,

Chapter 12: Building Meaningful Relationships With Influencers

Advertising to influencers is a critical part of your agency. Relationships are inside the middle of your professional achievement. Get it one step in addition, cultivate and hold relationships with folks who are influential on your Industry.

Influencer advertising and advertising and marketing is not a modern day way or technique of thinking. It has existed for a long time. Business proprietors have identified its fee for lots months and the way in which you make use of it is going to determine how profitable your business enterprise might be due to it.

You will discover loads of factors to do not forget almost about focused on influencers. The first problem is you need to perceive who the influencers are after which hyperlink with them so you can start to construct big; at the same time useful establishments with them.

An exciting issue can be that the folks who are categorised because the strongest influencers for you currently won't be the equal people in a while. Due to the short improvement of generation and the manner that influences companies nowadays, they're related to the gadget that is being carried out for corporation on a normal and constant time desk.

Generating influencer marketing and advertising and marketing and advertising need to be part of your famous net advertising and marketing technique You is probably capable of ask your self the purpose you desire to include influencer advertising for your advertising and marketing and advertising and marketing technique.

Needless to say, actually as traditional advertising and advertising and advertising is able to have a useful effect in your industrial company (and virtually want to), influencer marketing is able to get an further correct impact. The high amazing outcomes becomes apparent:

Making your influencers to interact

You should strive getting your influencers to create visitor weblog posts, get concerned with podcasts, and do interviews with you. That can serve severa functions. It is going to electrify others to recognize that your influencers help your industrial organization and accept as actual with on your services.

It'll preserve subjects charming and your efforts to hold to get sparkling, progressive thoughts to the table through your influencers will make people want to constantly be related to you and your industrial company.

Earning more hints on line

In case you could get your influencers to talk approximately you and your business organization on-line, thru their efforts, you may be strengthening your popularity and increase your exposure. Wherever you are mentioned isn't always just how often you are mentioned (as prolonged as it's in an terrific slight, of route).

Increase your web page site visitors

In case you could take benefit of their audiences, you'll be equipped to enhance the quantity of internet net web page website online visitors which incorporates you that could simply be a remarkable issue on your corporation.

Determining the importance of your business enterprise and your offerings

A remarkable technique to determine how useful you are to others is through the speakme that others voice among themselves. It's some thing that you sincerely see how useful your products and/or offerings are for lots distinctive human beings to recognize it. You are the best person who is now not accredited to voice the praises of your organization.

Earning credibility, trustworthiness, and promoting hundreds more

If you have were given the assist of the influencers using your employer, other individuals will take you severely, will bear in mind you sincere and credible, and could want to buy what you're selling.

Creating your dreams

There are many pastimes you have to have in thoughts for your business business enterprise earlier than you recognition on a few influencers, First of all, you want to installation precisely what you are trying to gain out of your advertising: You in reality need to have goals as a part of the advertising and advertising plan earlier than you select to do some aspect.

Those desires will hold you targeted and may assist you to gather success. Your desires will allow you to apprehend exactly which influencers are right for your business organization.

Develop a intention list: It is going to be less complicated than you be given as right with building a list of influencers. The right way to start is definitely thru performing a keyword seek and the influencers will appear within the consequences. There are many that can will will let you apprehend influencers.

You want to decide out how to make use of metrics because it want to be and it's far critical to recognize that an impressive rating isn't always the simplest essential identifying aspect close to deciding on influencers. When deciding on, you want to bear in mind the whole lot and then you could understand at the same time as that influencer is top notch for you.

Reach out: You must not anticipate to right away create a relationship with a sure influencer the number one time you speak with him. It is going to take a bit time (truely as it can with sincerely any dating). Keep in mind that relationships name for art work, being worried, nurturing, and a good buy of deliver and take.

Develop a first rate base: Before you begin the influencer marketing and advertising a part of your business business employer, you have to sense constant within the concept that you are beginning with a exceptional basis while it involves your agency as an entire.

When you've got all you could need and therefore are interacting together in conjunction with your influencer, make certain to paintings frequently at preserving the ones relationships and assisting them to expand.

Influencers are vital to the achievement of your business organisation. They will assist to enhance your on line reputation and they'll permit you to in the long run attain your goals of being seemed as an influencer in your employer or area of interest.

Remember to certainly be aware of what they are letting so you can mimic that if it simply works in your commercial enterprise. The relationships which you show your influencers want to be mutual, right, and certainly beneficial. Marketing is the high-quality and effective manner in your last business fulfillment.

Chapter 13: To Become An Influencer: Obtaining Fulfillment Through Team Behavior

All of it boils proper proper all the way down to the vital query - what is the which means that that of lifestyles?

In an try to collect the exceptional likely well worth due to this hassle, and located it at the market in our modern-day global, I are seeking advice from this query rather: what offers the entirety that means?

This particular inquiry may be reworded in plenty of distinct strategies to provide new views as properly: -What reasons you to experience enthusiastic as a person?

-What gives your lifestyles a enjoy of cause?

-How should we take the process that we do all through our lives, in maximum of our mind, the moves and the behaviors, and make use of this making our lives meaningful?

These questions and the look for his or her solutions may be placed on every element of our daily lives of. Particularly, considering them in relation to our place of business environment.

Having said that, how can we gain our personal achievement inside a enterprise corporation?

Certainly, the movement of asking those questions, many if no longer the majority of which have no unique responses, can be the number one movement that ought to attend to rethinking the framework of a revolutionary and powerful business enterprise.

A aware exam of our motives is probably useful not absolutely due to the achievement of our very very personal non-public success, however to assist us similarly realise the way to harness a real feel of reason in our lives and purpose that objective to spread to assist those spherical us.

From our cutting-edge international, generation makes it easy for every body to percentage what is on his mind and to connect those thoughts on a international scale. With a population of seven billion parents, we're faced with loads of suggestions!

The concept of getting an influencer, of starting motions, of creating and empowering tendencies, can be carried out thru effective group behavior. This is most significantly made viable through effective communique and robust control.

Today, allow us to take a step decrease decrease lower back from manage and personnel conduct, to better draw close the benefits an influencer performs in affecting a agency. An influencer can hold the interest as a pacesetter, so the leader functions as being a catalyst. The man or woman mind and reasons are what'll offer a particular imaginative and prescient or goal price.

Why-due to the truth the leader is not hesitant to step in advance and take motion.

Thus, whilst the use of the idea of management for a commercial enterprise employer, who need to step in advance as a pacesetter? Effectively, if the purpose is maximizing the productiveness of your agency, the solution is anybody.

Think of the overwhelming benefits of every and really all and sundry interior your enterprise both taking motion and speaking like a pacesetter. What is probably the results?

- Effective interaction of ideas, desires, and visions to one of a type individuals engaged in an progressive task

- The participation of every and every team of workers member in growing an essential method within the path of the attainment of your employer's desires

- Increased non-public duty in the path of unique movements and thoughts

- A more feel of cause Do you like looking outcomes? Let all people interior your enterprise have the creative freedom required to maximize his productiveness. Get rid of the reigns and permit the human beings inside your company to assume duty for his or her movements.

If definitely all of us indoors a commercial enterprise enterprise is authorized the progressive freedom to take rate and comprehend the goals of the organisation internal his very non-public way, does that beautify standard performance?

How approximately frame of employees morale? Performing this newfound experience of motive and mutual cooperation assist a personal developer as each a valued leader and member of the body of personnel?

If absolutely everyone internal your agency research non-public growth and could boom his productiveness-how does which have an impact on the group as an entire? This is the effect of group conduct within a enterprise enterprise. It impacts each person, and it starts offevolved with you.

Chapter 14: How You Can Effectively Deal With The Influencer

A lot of conditions in recent times come right down to pitching and seeking to have an effect on an influencer, it is time to train the appropriate manner of appearing it. A few topics initially.

An influencer is described as someone who is related to a way of you decide way - they often assist make the selection, or they need to approve your products or services to begin with earlier than they skip it onto other choice-makers, etcetera. The number one point proper proper right here is there can be any individual above them who weighs in severely or who is were given the very last say on inside the event that they've to waft in advance with you.

And so the primary issue you need to accomplish is to set up how your influencer works into the selection approach (if in any respect), and clearly how quite some affects they have got. Make use of the subsequent questions all through the qualification degree to set up this:

"And _____, except yourself, is there truely each person else who must weigh in in this?"

AND

"And so how does that approach paintings?"

AND

"What is your function in that manner?"

AND

"And truely how an awful lot impact do you've got in that device?"

AND

"What commonly occurs in case you recommend a few aspect like this?" ("Do they typically go with your advice?")

Occasionally you could have the potential to make it through every this form of mind in some unspecified time in the future of the qualification phase, but in case you could get rushed, ask around if you may. It is critical you have a wonderful concept of what your influencer's function is, and sincerely how hundreds of influences he has in advance than you circulate via your demo or employer presentation later.

By the way, at the same time as you begin your demo, it's miles commonly a clever choice going thru the ones questions again earlier than you release into your pitch. Doing this could provide you a head-up regarding how it is more likely to give up. Would now not or now not it's miles accurate to find out the stall in advance than it really pops up? And even as it could, right here is the way you address it:

You: "So from what we've lengthy long long gone over, it can sound this manner is an extraordinary healthy for you - we want to transport forward and get maintain of you beginning these days."

Influencer: "Well, I am going to want to illustrate this to the committee."

You: "I recognize, genuinely from hobby, depending on what you've got seen right here in recent times, do you without a doubt enjoy this may fit your needs (your organisation company, branch, and so on.)?"

Influencer: "Yes, it appears to be specific."

You: "Great, then you are probable to signify it to the committee?"

Influencer: "Yes I will."

You: "Good. Simply from hobby, what normally takes vicinity in case you take something to the committee that you in truth suggest?"

OR

You: "Good. Simply from hobby, if you take a few issue to the committee that you virtually recommend, what is going to they generally have a tendency to do?"

OR

You: "Great! And sincerely how a bargain effect do you have with what they'll emerge as doing?"

OR

You: "Great! And how often will they complement your recommendation?"

Note: If you get in the acquisition and they usually select out something they advise, then: You: "Wonderful! Because they usually take your recommendation, and because of the truth you're aboard with this, right right here is what I endorse we do: I will bypass on and get the agreement out for you and plan the date.

When you get the approval, we're able to have an entire lot of the activity finished to help you going. Today, what's a notable time for this assembly?"

Let us harm this down. The first trouble to do at the qualification degree is to get clarity over how hundreds effect your influencer had during the last preference. This is a critical step that many salespeople miss.

Then, in the end, you make certain the influencer changed into provided for your service or product to start with before you went down the "committee" course. It is crucial you got their buy in at this aspect.

After you get their buy in, that is even as you could ask if they will be probable to suggest it and the manner weighty their recommendation is. You could make this an ordeal near as you want, the element is which you desire to take your influencer as a protracted way as he goes to permit you to. The further they will can help you pass, the more likely they may be a deal later.

Begin making use of these strategies to your earnings calls to begin with the qualification section. The greater you find out approximately the influencer role, you may be better equipped you will be taking the near even in addition at the give up.

Chapter 15: What Makes A Good Influencer?

The capacity to persuade others is a totally beneficial. Influencers normally do speak a standard set of attitudes that ensure constant achievement. Creating a strong relationship with pals is important in influencing picks.

Due to that, we can say there may be a specific power if you want to consist of getting a power over them, however what will the strength implies in the absence of endure in mind? How can we earn their consider for us to prompt our capability to affect them? Allow me to share many clever strategies influencers set themselves to be effective:

Influencers factor out the rewards in their proposition] and placed a state of affairs or a state of affairs spherical those proposition for it to generate a big impact on the man or woman.

Influencers do Brand themselves.

Influencers are not simply marketers, allow us to confront the easy reality, the ones main influencers are a part of the tremendous industrial organization humans, they do now not splendid produce blogs thinking about they've web websites.

They do no longer genuinely have interaction in advertising and advertising because of the truth they might begin their private business corporation. Above all, they brand their private call. When you keep on with a particular industrial corporation or e a manufacturer, it's miles as if you have adhered to the face of that emblem or commercial enterprise enterprise.

Influencers analyze distinct alternatives to affect others; bespeak accelerated tiers of flexibility. For instance, an influencer desires to obtain a selected range of supporters on the stop of the month of September.

Even notwithstanding the fact that the final outcomes is an prolonged way too wonderful or did now not get to the preferred cause, what the influencer will do is looking for and test awesome techniques to enhance his lovers. Remember that an influencer with first rate flexibility ought to probably continuously manipulate some scenario.

They are their non-public Authors. Previously determined masses of on-line eBooks? Or a tangible e-book you located in your bookshelves. Those writers of the books could be the marketers themselves. The smooth fact that if an man or woman want to be one of the quality marketing influencers, you can decide to install writing a e-book within the long time. Why?

Being an Author may moreover provide quite some credibility in your very very very own logo. Besides, it's far hundreds to peer your call as an writer of a e-book? On the opportunity word, the ebook which an influencer can publish is but a few different form of branding. It similar to publishing and composing a ebook approximately the marketplace you're inquisitive about.

Influencers neutralize and foresee resistance ahead of time. They are capable of input a first rate affiliation to possible regions of that resistance.

Influencers are flexible.

These pinnacle influencers provide a whole lot of content, they certainly do it in some of unique techniques. I take delivery of as actual with it is an assumption any producers want to comply with. Note: As a producer, the greater stations you gain on, your reach receives wider which allows you to hyperlink with a number of people.

Every character is particular so influencers will discover what are the requirements and need of their audiences.

Influencers share its fortune. Top-rated influencers don't most effective sell, they assist and extends their assist past their customers and target audience. Leading advertising and marketing and marketing influencers additionally may be organized to speak approximately their knowledge, and in reality, some detail of that is strategic, because it extends the get right of access to of their message to new visitors.

Influencers voice out in advance than humans. The most effective advertising and advertising influencers are people who talk and show display themselves earlier than human beings. Blogging is an notable concept, prioritizing it a good way to percentage your very own mind is a simply powerful device to improve your influential competencies.

Thus, you desired to end up a fairly powerful influencer, right? Before that, you want to check out some gadgets that would can help you get going together along with your influencer adventure or in case you are presently an influencer, and also you felt you aren't effective sufficient to have an effect on others? Keep analyzing this monetary catastrophe, as it is going to help you and provide you with a number of mind to be an super influencer. Allow me to percentage the guidelines:

Be A Great Listener.

The one element a marketer or e salesperson do is being attentive to their customers for them to offer what the consumer truly want, or what and on the way to be the precise product to promote and promote to the purchaser.

As an influencer, you want to be aware of your friends with a view to formulate an entire lot better pointers for large impacts on their perception of you and the mission. I even have not heard everybody who were given harm with the resource of listening, have you ever ever? It is shape of hilarious, genuinely, listening will help you hundred % on the facet of your influencer recognition.

The More You Give, The greater you get keep of.

Don't expect that your peers will right now assist you at the side of your disasters. Running a business enterprise, there can be without a doubt nothing like "loose," you want to shop for if you want to acquire a few aspect super in change.

On a crew, in case you are seeing one in every of your teammates stopping, this can be a notable threat to help, offering them help will show that you are inclined to help them so each of you can have the capability to keep in mind the group achievement. In return, they'll assist you with what demanding conditions you're probably to come across and every of you could benefit from it.

Collaborations and partnerships.

Two minds are better than a unmarried one. Imagine, what and the vicinity are you going to be prepared to advantage on every occasion you and your personnel integrate your brains collectively, essentially combining your tips and mind together?

You will create amazing and incredible requirements! Open brainstorming will allow you to understand what your organization, is thinking. Surely, they've some trouble which may decorate the superb effect in your solutions, product, and advertising and marketing and advertising and marketing. Ending up on a worthwhile crew-up and better variations of approaches a great deal the frame of employees should arise one after the other.

These are the numerous tendencies and excellent hints to be a excellent influencer. You will find out scores of benefits to getting an influencer, but constantly take care, as you can discover primary rocks in every milestone you step upon doing paintings to your success as being an influencer.

Chapter 16: Building And Solidifying Your Relationships With Influencers

You have most likely heard a trouble about influencers. You may also have a chunk notion about what defines an influencer however your data won't pass out of doors of that. Something it absolutely is definitely critical to preserve in mind is the reality that influencers are critical to the fulfillment of your commercial company.

The first component which you want to accomplish is identifying who is an influencer and after that to pick out out the ideal influencers in your business company.

A awesome approach to start is by using the usage of manner of identifying the motive why a person has awesome impact over awesome people for your specific organization or place of hobby. Obviously, which influencer have to have finished top notch subjects which made him or her earn that influencer circumstance. Originating from an advertising and advertising and advertising attitude, there are some regions which might be probably the most visible and most critical.

Reach: Your obtain is described because the style of oldsters which you have the possibility to link with (on any real degree) with the influencer. Undoubtedly, you can just like those folks which may be treasured to your organisation.

Relevance: When you're within the use of figuring out the influencers which can be in all likelihood the maximum beneficial on your business company, the numerous the use of factors is critical.

If what the influencer is doing or pronouncing has no hyperlinks with what you are trying to do together with your agency, the chances are useful the man or woman will not be the perfect influencer for you individually.

On the opportunity hand, if the individuals' technique is synergistic with what you are trying to do collectively at the side of your business corporation, he or she's maximum in all likelihood a brilliant in form for you.

Resonance: At this degree in the task, you have got got truly recognized your aim marketplace and you're growing those relationships. Whichever influencer(s) you've got got were given labeled because the most appropriate ones in your corporation, that individual's suggestions need to resonate no longer actually with you but together with your target marketplace.

In case the information does now not resonate with every person involved, you could want to target your influencer improperly.

Determine your social media influencers

It's not usually simple to determine who's the greatest social media influencers to your enterprise business enterprise. Logically talking, you need to make certain that the influencers who you have identified for your commercial enterprise commercial enterprise company are in truth the precise options. During the technique of identifying those influencers, maximum of the topics that you could likely want to test out are the massive sort of people that follow that influencer and the vicinity that the person ranks on the net seek engine internet web sites.

In terms of the large sort of fans, there are clean techniques wherein you could do that, based totally on the particular social networking channels that you are analyzing.

If you're reading a specific influencer, you want to test him or m her out on social networking channels like Facebook, Google+, LinkedIn, and Twitter. All of them are going to allow you to recognize the extensive form of connections which an influencer has.

Those social networking channels will assist you to get a first-rate sense of techniques involved that specific influencer is with many other human beings on-line. That is but every other detail that is vital for you even as you're choosing an influencer. A part of that engagement is going to be inside the form of element and "likes" of it'll be a actual dialogue.

Your studies goes to let you determine out now not clearly at the same time as the influencer is a subject rely range professional however if the person is a person with who you really want to attach on a person stage.

search engine optimization is but a few other very crucial issue of your preference. In case the influencer does no longer rank on the pinnacle of the hunt engine internet pages, you'll possibly ought to reconsider your choice.

The search engine positions are clearly essential and any man or woman that thinks it is no longer needed to supply interest to that is doing his employer a huge disservice. You will see with time it surely is the extra top amazing content material you percentage online, the more your seek engine scores can be.

Take observe of the engagement component

To be capable of pick out the correct social media influencers, you can want getting to recognize them first. That technique that you want to have interaction with them. You will need to start beneficial interactions (or, at minimal, a tremendous one) together with the influencer, therefore, you absolutely get to find out what he stands for. Whenever the man or woman's views are not truly a fit if you want to promote, it will no longer advantage your company.

If you start the communication, make certain you offer a few element of worth to the alternative person. It is probably a big mistake that you can preserve out for the opportunity individual to offer price first. If you start this, you can have a little manipulate with the relationship, and that is what you would really like.

Generally, the alternative person is going to react undoubtedly to what you are questioning. That's exactly how you assemble the connection (and preferably it's miles going to be a protracted lasting one).

If your content material cloth is valuable to the influencer, he or she goes to talk about your articles with others. Again, it's far honestly what you would really like to expose up. Which increases your attain and your relevance. It'll increase your seek engine rankings.

Keep strong connections with influencers

At this level, you have got executed a whole lot of labor to ensure that you solidify the reference to your influencer(s). In a nutshell, you have were given assisted the muse for the connection. Nevertheless, your courting in conjunction with your influencers (similar to all relationships) dreams remedy.

Establishing your relationships is important and it's far really vital. Nevertheless, you'll input the renovation level of the connection. To be capable of hold those relationships, you need to interact on a everyday time table. You will need to seize the statistics of who your influencers are in a manner.

Creating lists may work pretty well for that. Even even though it won't set you decrease again a penny to maintain the ones relationships, there might be an essential purchase at the a part of yours. You will want to dedicate effort and time.

Which ought to be pretty easy to do need to you're making the willpower. All things taken into consideration, it is your business enterprise and you may need to do the whole thing viable to be as effective as feasible.

Influencers are very essential for your achievement. The equal as another essential human relationships, you want to set the connection, amplify it, and maintain it proper. You receives a remarkable pass again to your funding

Like every a sizeable thing in every day existence, relationships with influencers require work but are properly well well worth the effort. As time evolves, you want to keep in mind that you need to be flexible in conjunction with your market and the humans with who you talk those forms of important, influential interactions.

Chapter 17: Influencers, Brand Advocates, Brand Ambassadors,

These three phrases are not unusual nowadays and are applied despite the fact that you want to recognise that asides spellings, further they have got variations within the impact and region they are in.

What are the specialists and cons in case they may be used? What do they truly do for a logo? These are the insights you could find in this unique monetary disaster. Let us smash them down extra further:

Influencers

They are human beings which have have an effect on. They have their private one-of-a-kind requirements, the diameter of subjects and feature an impact on of interest. Their reach might be compact or vast even though its hundred % certain that you can gather your investments decrease back over one hundred %, it truly is pleasant due to their "have an impact on."

They may go with you or now not, but, they could have the capability to have an effect on their target market about your brand, why? Since they're actually certainly one of your clients!

Celebrities which incorporates Selena Gomez, Kardashians, and masses of others. Are the diverse historically most main and top notch influencers, specially within the style employer. Though these days, bloggers are maximum of the maximum influential people...

Brand call Ambassadors

They additionally love influencers, despite the fact that they have been hired for a long term dating, they may be the face of the enterprise or business enterprise they may be in. Influencers are simply able to brief term campaigns. Brand ambassadors have complete statistics approximately the logo and are loud and thrilled with their ambassadorship at some point of their channels.

They are the professionals that relate to the brand, its product, and services. Those spokespeople which are working out of doors the commercial organization enterprise moreover can be taken into consideration as any celebrities and emblem Ambassadors or influencers underneath agreement and feature a producer is a Brand Ambassador.

Brand name Advocates

They are your maximum trustworthy and rigorous patron. They can be your, shareholders, and companions employees. They are those who speak approximately their satisfaction and reports collectively with your products or logo and obviously, it's miles continuously free,

All the ones customers which can be giving and publishing feedback in your commentary sections or evaluation thing might be the Brand Advocates, They can be influencers, via influencing their co clients regarding your product.

Nevertheless, the strategies wherein the ones severa agencies are monitored and maintained, are congruent. This is why human beings are far satisfied the future of advertising is an effective and flexible platform that might supply all the tool that companies should control and optimize types of tasks.

Influencer Marketing is critical for producers' advertising and advertising and marketing as influencers are critical in visiting engagements and recruiting new site visitors.

The preliminary step of Influencer desire is knowing the primary versions in these specific categories in your brand. On the turn thing, manufacturers want to create a narrowed dreams and method for his or her campaigns as a manner to confirm and pick the effective and right influencer on your logo.

Chapter 18: Why You Need To Hire Influencers

Why might you want to lease influencers to sell your organization?

The problem commonly pops up in speak with new employer, and those might also moreover ask yourself why in reality all and sundry may pay' the huge dollars' to find out the right marketing strategist on their organisation.

Influencers revel in a immoderate effect to be had available in the marketplace, and in case they will be targeted to your location of interest, it's miles YOUR vicinity of hobby they have got an effect on. Hire influencers due to the reality that they have an impact available available on the market vicinity for your pick!

Thus why must you lease influencers to sell your commercial enterprise on-line?

Social media Marketing

You lease influencers to supply large impact over your commercial enterprise on social networking at the grounds that they've an impact you may no longer have someplace else.

Numbers, material, and people with very excessive levels of effect on mass media are related.

They hook as plenty as many human beings, as others rate what they've to say and listen. It sincerely makes a distinction in the style of people are listening.

Content Marketing Strategies

Important people force crowds with their phrases. They create persuasive, compelling message geared to fascinating a market. The target audience will become your goal market because of the reality you associated with and lease influencers. Consequently, the final effects is income to your pocket from conversion advertising.

Keyword Optimized Content

Important marketers realize the advantages of producing noticeably polished, key-phrase-optimized, articles which push visitors for the purpose that they need plenty of visitors to keep their crowd marketing programs.

Crowd advertising and marketing hovers near content material fabric material material due to the fact it's miles loaded to the brim with specific strategies. You require written content material cloth fabric. You want to have techniques. Solution-primarily based completely written content material is expected each time you rent influencers.

Compelling Calls to Action

Influential income reps recognize the way to close to the sale. They completely hold near the functionality of having the client to the market and last the gap just so they can not leave.

An influential sales rep goes to bring in massive quantities of properly-focused opportunities and promote the item, services, or connections. The simplest outcomes are available from automatic conversion practices. The approach will art work.

Hire Influencers to advertise

Obviously, you are not going to employ honestly all of us to sell your agency. You will want a person in your industry, or this is aware about your market in processes an excellent way to entice clients internal your area of hobby.

Who you hire to market your business agency subjects, and what they do to marketplace your commercial enterprise. The key element is knowing who to appoint, for truly how an entire lot, and why you require that particular person. Then placing that individual on the rack to get the way accomplished.

Chapter 19: The 4 Influencers In A B2b Sale

You will find 4 classes of humans you need to be aware about B2B earnings. All those businesses - it can be just one man or woman at in reality any of the agencies, nearly about the scale of the industrial employer - has an impact on whether or not or not you may near the sale or not.

To disregard any man or woman of those affects will most probable endorse you could not make the purchase. This is the actual distinction amongst B2B sales and purchaser profits. An enterprise sale receives to be extra complicated, as each any such influencing authorities very personal agendas, they require content cloth.

All those groups of humans are laid low with how your products or services will have an effect on them in their manner. They are searching at how your services or products will right now have an impact on their enterprise business enterprise.

They need to find out if they'll be truely making the ideal choice for themselves and their business agency. They do not actually need to damage their career, and in case you can help them to decorate their career, you then certainly might be an extended manner within the front of any competition.

Simply due to the fact you have to influence masses of human beings in a B2B transaction, this is the number one cause the advertising and marketing cycle takes so very extended.

These four impacts are.

1. The Financial Influence(s)

2. The User Influences

three. The Gatekeeper(s)

four. Your Sponsor or Champion

1. The Financial Influence(s)

Each of them is important, and each of them performs a truly essential characteristic in whether or not their business enterprise will purchase from you.

We will have a look at the number one one on the listing, The Financial Influencer, or as I want to cellular telephone name him - The Cheque Signer, or The closing Authority. This is the maximum essential individual to should discover. This need to be the primary person you contact on every occasion you are attempting to open a ultra-modern account.

Often times we touch a person anybody apprehend in an account, and frequently instances they will be the owners of our products or services. We sincerely have to find out those oldsters moreover, however if you begin within the pinnacle, subsequent you may continuously return to them in some time in the product earnings cycle.

When you begin with any person beneath this influencer on the commercial enterprise chart, then you'll have a totally, ough time trying to gain this authority and influencer in a while in the product income cycle, even as you might have to speak to him.

Let's take a look at the economic influencer, and find out what inclinations this unique person has, and why this specific man or woman is so important to understand.

The economic influencer's feature is giving the ultimate approval to shop for. This function may be made from many people. It might be an government committee. It is probably the Board of Directors. Much of the location goes to rely upon a choice of variables. The 3 maximum terrific elements for you're:

1. The scale of the commercial enterprise company

2. The dollar amount of your perception

3. The impact your solution has on the organisation

You will discover the amount of motives for why this influencer can be a committee. Probably the most crucial element of the buying technique is the aspect that impacts your services or products has on the economic organization.

Chapter 20: Advocates Or Influencers, Where Should You Invest?

There is an lousy lot speak now concerning "INFLUENCERS" and surely how organizations need to build an navy of those humans to help you beautify their logo. Can it's genuine or the proper trouble to do?

Should you invest cash into this particular marketing and approach tactic?

Allow me to provide an opportunity perspective that you may think approximately before you dive into this particular approach.

I recollect it is essential to smooth up one element it truely is usually stressed... The huge difference amongst an ADVOCATE. And an INFLUENCER Sometimes those terms get used interchangeably and to me, they're fantastic people.

An INFLUENCER is a person who will help persuade and feature an impact on some different person's opinion almost about a organization business business enterprise's product, software, and expertise.

They may moreover or not use the goods or offerings or maybe had an journey together with the enterprise first hand but primarily based surely upon their function in the marketplace their opinion subjects over others. In many times, in addition they may be compensated in a manner for their have an impact on and opinions over prospective customers.

For instance, let's do not forget any individual is acquainted with a particular services or products based totally mostly on their research in a particular vicinity. They can also moreover write about this precise object and claim that based absolutely mostly on the research of theirs it seems to be an excellent product and one issue they will advocate to others. Because they'll be official of their enterprise, they're viewed as absolutely everyone who can communicate with authority.

There are additional instances of influencers as properly... Like personnel which may be operating in your organisation. They can say how exquisite it's miles strolling how and there outstanding the humans are and what incredible visionaries the leaders seem to be and so on.

They are "influencing" the goal market on the grounds that they've "insider" information concerning how matters feature. You will discover associated instances even though they nearly all very personal the same motive... To have an effect on you in a way and so the commercial agency sticks out from the organization and you can optimistically purchase their products or services.

Chapter 21: Why Does A Brand Require Influencers?

Influencers are the ones people which can be lively on social networking and blogs. They are a topic and logo advocates promoter. But why are they essential in your brand?

Why does the emblem need your influencers? Here is why:

The customers or consumers get hold of as actual with suggestions from a 3rd celebration, more often compared to a logo name itself. Admit it, you can't consider in a person in a party that comes up amazingly for you and brags approximately himself and their individual, in reality to persuade you to be their friend.

Social media, its explosive and big boom in the closing years produced a trade in how corporations & producers use advertising. The famous techniques of pushing out branded records on your goal market? That's not as effective because it was.

The customers have the maximum electricity because of social networking and they count on to take part with makes in "actual-time". Nowadays, conventional advertising techniques take the rear seat to new techniques, the ones new techniques preserve clients engaged and attracted while retaining on driving them to behave. It's a genius approach.

The concept and techniques of influencer advertising and advertising are becoming tremendous stuff for all of the entrepreneurs, it can start new avenues which you can link up collectively together along with your customers without delay.

The strength of social impact maintains developing, social media clients with plenty of affects may be more important to your emblem than one-of-a-kind sorts of a paid ad. Although it takes effort and time to execute, it's truly well worth each penny.

Influencer Marketing Increases your Credibility

While growing your authority by using using collaborating with vital human beings, you can clearly grow your emblem's gain. You produce the content you would love, rank better on on-line are looking for for engine results pages and be green on social networking, do now not have credibility.

Important clients accept as true with their pals or networks over every unique emblem and this is the cause an influencer point out is capable of offer you a quick song to credibility. Put really, you've got got examined your feature with the authoritative presence of the promoter.

The idea of Influencer Marketing Can help you Broaden The Audience of yours.

Take the time to decide the correct influencers who'll in form your logo or those who influential customers who have the equal pursuits as your logo call will enchantment to a larger market. Collaborating with them offers you with access to a whole lot of audiences which have a big ability to be consumers of your merchandise.

Can help you With your seek engine marketing and advertising and marketing.

If the written content cloth is produced, influencers will truely hyperlink once more on your net page by means of way of generating a inbound link. This system is a well-known clean reality which the amount of referring one-way links and domains for your internet website capabilities a powerful effect for your personal on line searching for engine effects page or SERP rankings.

Drives Lead and Boost Sales.

The big your collect is, it's far a large benefit of influencer advertising and marketing. Besides on that concept, product income and outcomes will hold the logo's adventure hold.

Developing your influencer offer a discount code to their audiences is an top notch method to encourage individuals to buy your product. Clearly, at the surrender of the morning, the income will exceed greater than what you anticipate.

In every Marketing Strategy, it's far masses important which you decide key typical overall performance signs and signs and symptoms and determine them after your approach becomes activated.

Chapter 22: The Best Way To Choose The Right Influencer For Your Brand

Influencers have grow to be the top celebrities in the worldwide. Because of social networking, influencers have grown to be the critical nucleus which connects clients and brands.

With regards for your emblem image, permit the arena apprehend what your corporation stands for, what it method to folks which can be a part of it--influencers play the main feature.

In the existing digital age, it's far influencers which determine the results of your agency and this is why choosing the excellent one is important to the development of your organization.

The rather effective area of hobby-primarily based content material they produce is centered strictly in the route of persuading just appealing with clients. Whether or now not you seeking out mommies, foodies price range travelers, fashionistas, or coffee drinker influencer kinds to assist the business, their advertising and marketing and advertising wants to paintings.

Below are a few tips on what you want to do to advantage the consequences you need:

Look for commonplace values and hobby.

It's critical for the clients of yours to feel like they may be part of some factor right. What this means is your influencer need to be in a characteristic to illustrate that he believes to your commercial enterprise product.

Customer engagement empathy. Look on the numbers. The influencer you pick wishes to be a person who have to have interaction with clients day and make them enjoy as they are part of a massive family.

It isn't hard to select one enterprise employer with the opportunity despite the fact that the purpose is getting the customer to find out why they want to just accept as real with on your emblem and why your issuer is credible enough to shop for it.

Select relevance over the rest.

The influencer should be a taking walks instance of your emblem persona type. As a consumer, you may need to create a selection which speaks for you and represents who you're.

For instance, you may now not need to buy a musical device from a employer with Bill Gates because of the truth the influencer or a musical device from a organisation with Beyonce as its influencer.

It is absolutely essential to choose out influencers who will increase the financial organisation growth with their lovers. If the influencer includes followers in hundreds of lots but simply 10 people engage together with his recurring content material, it might not be worthwhile to hassle. Do now not allow impressions, clicks, and lovers pressure your desire. You is probably throwing out coins on nugatory advertising if you are doing that.

Do your due diligence.

An terrific influencer sparks interest with each posting by the use of manner of engagement. Their content material is virtually ordinary, effective and turns campaigned site visitors into conversions and leads, giving your emblem the increase it requires.

www.ingramcontent.com/pod-product-compliance
Lightning Source LLC
LaVergne TN
LVHW022315060326
832902LV00020B/3473